CHEEZIER

BY FIRE CHAPLAIN STEVEN J.
" CHEESEBURGER" STRUBLE

To Devin
Fire chaplain
cheese

SJS

Editing, formatting, and cover by Kyle Marie McMahon of Literatus Editing & Prose

DEDICATION

This book is dedicated to my Lord and Savior Jesus Christ!

To my family, friends, and all the people who have made me cheezier, I pray each of y'all find blessings, hope, and peace in Jesus Christ.

CONTENTS

A FIREFIGHTER'S PRAYER

When I put on my gear Lord, please help me be courageous and protective, serving my community. If I should have to risk my life, help me to be brave, give me wisdom, give me strength when there are lives to save, remind me why I chose this work and to fulfill the call, remind me that You are here with me and watching over all. and when the day is over Lord, most of all I pray, that I will come home to those I love safely every day. Amen.

I have been given permission to use and mention the calls in this book. While I was trying to honor my role as a firefighter chaplain, I was also trying to keep many calls I have been on hidden. God brought many of them more into the light. This book is not meant to hurt or insult anyone. This is my story.

INTRODUCTION

Well, here I am, once again, on the scene. When my first book, *Cheezey*, was released in the fall of 2022, many people asked me, "Chaplain Cheese, when is the sequel coming out?!" Well here it is, and not to worry, I am still cheezey. If you have not read *Cheezey* or never met me, allow me to introduce myself. My name is Firefighter Chaplain 79 Steven J. "Cheeseburger" Struble. And yes, I am a Christian!

I never really wanted the spotlight. Just give me my wintergreen mints and dispatch me to whatever calls I am needed at, and I am cheezey (to all my new readers, "cheezey" means good). But so many of my family and friends were spreading the word about my book. (Thank y'all so much!) We did a book signing event on the second day of Pineville Fall Fest and ended up with a pretty great crowd! Some people had gotten there before it started and did not leave until after I left. I lost my mind when my mama surprised me with Ms. Rummage and two of my Utah nieces and nephews, Aubrey and Gavin! I hadn't seen them since we visited in 2019 (what is with seeing my Utah family every five years). And boy did I need that.

So many people think writing a book is easy. Ha! Wrong! There is so much time and effort that goes into it. Not just writing it, but promoting it. I was having to deal with more than book stuff. I was also focusing on running my lawn service, running chaplain calls, handling church stuff, and learning how to drive with my permit. There was so much planning, but my editor kept me patient and my mama, family, and friends helped me out.

I started on this book in the summer of 2023 because of a Life Lesson Sermon I had written (I will get to the sermon part later). I also had a lot of people giving me advice on what to write: "Make your book about Life Lesson Sermons. Make your book about the SOUTH! Make your book about calls you have been on." And these are great topics that mean a lot to me.

This year, I felt like I was being backed into a corner. And it is not really a good idea to back an autistic person into a corner, especially an autistic person who is a firm believer in our Lord and Savior Jesus Christ! Can I please get an Amen?!

I have been bullied all my life. People question my ability to do my job or handle certain situations. They question if I can handle the stress of being an ordained volunteer firefighter chaplain. They question if I am able to take lead on the church security team. They even question if I have been called by God to be a church deacon. Yes, I am the one sitting in front of my laptop in the late hours, writing that Life Lesson Sermon, but it was God who was typing through me.

As I said in my Life Lesson Sermon, "I am Cheezey," you can try to lock me in a cage and try to put a brand-new style on me, but I've been cornered before, and I did not go speechless the last time and I certainly will not go speechless this time. I will do what I always do, wear what I want to wear, lift my hands up to Heaven, bow my head, soar and burn across the sky on the wings of an eagle who is also my Lord and Savior Jesus Christ, and remain cheezey!

Once again, my commander and chief, Jesus Christ, who is also my Lord and Savior, is pushing me and calling me to share another book.

As it says in 1 Timothy 4:11-16:

> Command and teach these things. Let no one despise your youth; instead, you should be an example to the believers in speech, in conduct, in love, in faith, in purity. Until I come, give your attention to public reading, exhortation, and teaching. Do not neglect the gift that is in you; it was given to you through prophecy, with the laying on of hands by the council of elders. Practice these things; be committed to them, so that your progress may be evident to all. Pay close attention to your life and your teaching; persevere in these things, for by doing this you will save both yourself and your hearers.

Firefighter Chaplain 79 to Central, Firefighter Chaplain 79 is on scene.

LEAVING PINEVILLE FIRE

In the middle of 2021, I was considering leaving my old department. I spoke with Lieutenant Firefighter Chaplain Tommy Nieman, who is not only a friend but a brother and mentor I met through the fire service. I speak to Tommy often, mostly through weekly check-ins and if I need guidance, encouragement, or even a prayer. He said he would support me in my decision but reminded me that I am still a firefighter chaplain, with or without a department. Through Tommy, God made sure my head was screwed on tight.

Tommy encouraged me to stay in contact with the Pineville Fire Department and my fellow brothers and sisters, visiting and checking in from time to time. He also reminded me that even if I am an inactive volunteer firefighter chaplain for a department like Pineville, I am still a firefighter chaplain for Christ and my community.

An active firefighter chaplain means you are a member of a department, helping out with station duties, training, running calls, and other things like leading worship service. Being an inactive firefighter chaplain just means you are not fully committed to one department. You still check in with your fellow brothers and sisters as well as civilians. I am an inactive firefighter chaplain. I mostly focus on the spiritual side of things and go where the Spirit of the Lord tells me or leads me, or when I am called to a scene or asked to help someone in need.

When on scene or taking care of an emergency situation, you need gear. On a fire scene, there may be smoke you don't want to inhale or other chemicals that can get on your skin.

Even on non-fire scenes, gear is important. Back when I was active, we were coming home from the beach and came upon the scene of a motorcycle accident. I still remember seeing all of the blood! There had been a fatality, and I was asked to pray for the fallen family member on a busy highway. I only had my Bible and vest. Bunker pants would have been better to have, as I was kneeling. The chief on scene said if I had had my gear, I could have started putting oil dry out and helping clean up the accident scene.

When I left Pineville Fire, I gave all the gear back except for items that I bought or were given to me by others. I kept my old firefighter flashlight in the car as well as a first aid med bag and a safety vest. I had my old turnout bag in my room because I did not want to take up too much space in my mama's car. I don't have a truck yet, still saving for it and insurance. Whenever I get my truck one day, I will have some emergency firefighter dashboard lights, as well as fire chaplain and storm chaser decals. (I cannot wait for my truck, because I am going further into the core to chase the tornado!)

My mama and I learned the hard way that I needed to keep my firefighter helmet in her car, especially when there are thunderstorms and tornadoes in the area. The only thing I have for gear is some turnout bunker boots and gloves, my Nomex hood, my radio strap, window punchers, service knives, and my Bible.

THE CHAPLAIN CALL

In November of 2021, I received a chaplain call. It was one that had a lasting impact on me.

But before I get into it, I have to give you a little background. When someone calls 911, Central answers it. They listen to the person on the phone, summon Pineville Fire (or whoever is needed), and relay what is going on at the scene. We could have a whole truck load or just a two- or three-man crew. A lot of times I got to ride on the engine. I even rode on the ladder with Captain Herman and Captain Clark.

There is a lot of communication on calls. Now some guys already know the plan and what they are going to do, and that is cool. I was told by my fire chief, Mike Gerin, to listen to either him, the deputy chief, or one of the assistant chiefs. If they were not there, the officer in charge would be in command. If we were on scene at car wrecks, I was told to lay down oil dry or grab a broom and sweep up the glass and debris off the road. If we were on fire scenes, I was to grab a Halligan bar, stand by or catch the hydrant, help lay hose line or prepare the squad to run, or refill air bottles. A few times I hit mini fires with water cans and extinguishers. Sometimes I hit it with the hose.

Whenever I would go on calls with Pineville Fire, I would gear up, riding on an engine or whatever truck was available to get on. Sometimes I would just have my bunker pants on, my radio (if there were some available) slung across my chest attached to my radio strap, and my helmet. But more often, I would be fully geared up with my bunker pants, turnout gloves, Nomex hood, and radio with the mic tucked outside of my turnout coat.

There is no such thing as a routine call! I will say it again in case people do not hear me: *There is no such thing as a routine call.* The thing about chaplain calls is that sometimes they are tougher than the ones you go on riding in a truck. Many people think my job is easy, or that my job is not a big deal. Well, it is a big deal! Often, I have no personal protective equipment on me!

Often firefighters, especially chaplains, do not carry radios with them—especially the ones that are inactive. The only form of communication we have are our prayers we lift up to God and the ones we send out on a cell phone. Active911 is a tool many departments use. It is a device on your phone or laptop that alerts the department and its members of calls, meetings, training, or group chats. Each member of the department is assigned a code to be on it. When I left Pineville Fire, I deactivated my Active911.

So when I received this chaplain call, the only thing I had on me was my cell phone and service knife—as well as my spiritual armor. On this call, some events arose that forced me go above and beyond the call of duty.

The individual I was ministering to was contemplating suicide. I'll call him Gentle Giant. No one knew I was alone with him or even that I was in the house. I gave him the Words of Jesus Christ, but I saw we were getting nowhere. Gentle Giant was in a very dark place and red flares had gone up, so I requested advice from someone close to him. I followed the advice I was given and then alerted 911. Within a few seconds, I found myself initiating my first Mayday call.

So, if you have never heard the term Mayday, it is a radio codeword we use for an emergency. It alerts people to let them know, "Hey, I am in distress." In the fire service—or at least in Pineville—we are taught to say, "Mayday. Mayday. Mayday. Firefighter down." Central will acknowledge and clear radio traffic. Then we state our LUNAR information. It is an acronym we use to help us remember what to tell Command. It stands for (examples in parentheses):

Location (Third floor)

Unit (Ladder Company 18)

Name (Firefighter John Doe)

Air Supply (Low on my SCBA bottle)

Resources Needed (Ladder on the Charlie side for window bailout)

I was able to retrieve and locate the firearm, and by the grace of God, I was able to get out of the house without injury. (I still got a little burned up on the mental part, but I am cheezey.) I alerted Central to notify fellow first responders of what was happening and tell them that a fire chaplain was on scene, but it was Cheeseburger. First responders I had worked with many times—some of whom were my fellow brothers and sisters of fire and police—came and took over the scene and patient care. When asked, I told them no one else was in the house.

I was seated in Officer TJ Whitley's squad car, and some of the Pineville firefighter guys, including Jon Clary, approached me to ask if I was okay. Some of them wanted to follow procedure and wanted me to get checked out, but I told them I was good and that I did not want anybody to know about this.

I was taught that when a firefighter (or any other branch of service member) is injured or dies on scene, their family will be notified. Mama and I talked about it because I was planning on going more into it with Pineville Fire. She asked, "If you ever got seriously hurt or if for whatever reason you die, how would I be told?" Depending on how serious it is, they will send a squad car along with a chaplain and your department chain of command. My case was serious enough that they would send another firefighter chaplain and my fire chief.

If they sent two uniforms over to Carmel Middle School where Mama worked at the time and she saw them without me, she is going to think there had been a line of duty death or I am missing in action. I said, "Y'all are not putting her through that. If we are going to do this, we are going to do it my way. Not yours, my way!"

I called the school phone and told them I needed to speak with Mama. and it could not wait. People were used to me calling. They even asked what was wrong. They heard the officers and my fellow firefighters in the background. All I told Mama was that I responded to a fire chaplain call and the person was having one of these moments. That's it.

People still question that, and I'll go into it more in a later chapter, but at the time, I had more work to do. I had to notify next of kin. I did the best I could to keep calm, but when next of kin started asking questions, I had to let Officer Whitley take over.

We came back to the scene and the officers were still clearing the house. I had told everyone there was no one else inside, but I knew TJ was someone I could really trust, not just because he was an officer, but because he is a fellow disciple of Jesus Christ. I know most of the guys there are Christians, but I knew Officer TJ would understand this information quicker.

I told him that during the chaos that went on in the house, I felt someone holding me. It was God. God was holding me! Yes, the God of all creation, the One who became fully human but was still fully God and who was Jesus Christ, came and held me in that hallway. It was a faceoff against the Devil himself holding Gentle Giant while God the Father held me. Yes, I saw the Devil, at least his eyes and smile. The pressure I felt was not a tight hold but rather a protective embrace of love that could only be given by Jesus Christ. He was holding me and said to the Devil, "You may have one of My children right now. But you will not have this child."

Now, I'm not saying Gentle Giant is not a Christian, because I believe wholeheartedly that he is a Christian, 100 percent. The only difference is that Gentle Giant felt chained down, when in reality, Jesus Christ has released him from all of the chains and wants him to know that God loves him, even when he is not so gentle.

After I said said this, TJ's face lit up. And I was like, "TJ, I am not crazy!" I knew if I had told anybody else, they would have tried to lock me up in some kind of mental place.

I was given a no contact order due to the events of that day, which I think as a firefighter chaplain is unfair. I felt like I was being blocked from doing what God wanted me to do. I can still talk to Gentle Giant on the phone, but I cannot see him without a supervisor on scene—and I still do not understand that. But you know what, there is a lot that I do not understand, but I am still cheezey.

I went home and showered and went to bed and let my emotions flow out of me. Many of my fellow first responders were calling me, texting me, some even driving by. Some I am grateful for reaching out. I even went to lunch with some of them and we talked about the events of that day. But some that called, I was hurt even more. Because when I needed their help back in a different part of my life, they were nowhere to be found. There were a lot of emotions on this call. Some of these people wanted to help, but my trust was still breached, and the only person I trusted was God. I do not have PTSD (post-traumatic stress disorder), but I did have questions, and I needed answers. But I would not get those answers until later.

I know many still do not know about this, and honestly, I am done apologizing and trying to justify my actions! Yes, I did perform actions to save another individual's life at the price of almost losing my own. YES! For almost a whole year I kept this in. I talked about it with some fellow firefighters and police officers that were there on scene, but to my family, church, and friends, I had not mentioned it. The only thing they knew was what I told Mama. I was so wrapped up in my new book that I was able to put it away deep inside me and lock it down somehow.

If you have to ask me why and how I did that, I have three reasons:

1. To spare the people I love the pain of seeing what I see during chaplain calls or any other fire calls I go on. This was my first call with a suicide attempt, and I knew it would not be my last one. But I did not know how close the first one would be to my second one.

2. Two things I live by are honor and loyalty. Without that there can be no trust. I am a firefighter chaplain, and I pray with many people. I cannot give out personal information. I do not go on people's Facebook and announce what we are praying for or what they are going through. I kept this down deep for a whole year, and I would have gone until my death with it.

3. God saw I needed time to heal, time to breathe, time to reflect and recharge. But also time to prepare me for a future that would be very dark, and a blessing that would make no sense.

THE PINEVILLE POLICE BANQUET

A few weeks before Mama, Nana, Tim, and I went to the beach for my birthday (like we do every year), I got a call from TJ to see if I would come to the Pineville Police Banquet. Of course I was going to attend to support the police officers and other staff members of the department. They asked me if I would pray over the meal. At first, I thought they were up to something. They said, "Make sure you invite Mama Cheese."

It was Class A uniform attire. Since I had given most of my stuff back and did not have a lot of money, I went on Amazon and bought a Class A shirt. Unfortunately, my fire chaplain badge and name plate would not come until the day after the banquet. At least I still had my Class A pants, shoes, uniform tie, and my fire rank chaplain pins that were given to me by fellow firefighter chaplain Frank Honaker when I made department chaplain in Pineville Fire.

The banquet was on October 4, 2022, at the Pineville Hut. Mama had gotten off work late (she is retired now!), so we arrived a little later. Officer Randy and his wife and children were by the front door. He said, "We have you both a seat on the right side of the room with one of our Pineville members. You are up next, get ready."

I said, "Yes sir," then smiled and handed him my tie. "Could you please help tie my tie?" I am still trying to learn how to. I do not feel bad about not knowing how because there are many people who do not know how to tie a tie.

My name was called to pray for the meal. The food was amazing, and the banquet had so many awards for so many outstanding officers and others. I even got to see a lot of my fellow brother and sister officers and supporters as well as some of the Pineville police chaplains, including my great friend Reverend Tim Jones.

Then it happened.

I was shocked to hear Officer TJ Whitley relay the events of the night in late November 2021, when I was on scene with Gentle Giant. Then he called my name. TJ and Pineville Police Chief Hudgins presented me with the Civilian Commendation Award.

Of course I said thanks, especially to Chief and TJ, but I also said I don't deserve it. I saw a person in trouble, and I acted. I don't deserve an award for it . . .

I went back to my table and Mama was looking at me with what I thought was disappointment. She said what was on her mind. I think she got over it. I even tried to justify myself, but I shouldn't have to.

THE FALLOUT

Jesus says in John 15:12-13,

> *This is My command: Love one another as I have loved you.*
> *No one has greater love than this, that someone would lay*
> *down his life for his friends.*

As the night went on, my phone was going off like the Fourth of July. Mama had said something like, "You know Nana is going to want to hear this before she finds out from someone else."

The Pineville Police Banquet was streamed on Facebook Live. I do not have Facebook (thank the Lord), but people were calling, congratulating me and telling me how proud they were. Some people did the opposite, saying, "What were you thinking?! You do not put your life on the line or go to that kind of call without back up! You could had been shot or killed!"

This was how I wanted to respond to those comments: "You think I don't know that?! You don't think I was scared when I saw and heard Gentle Giant make comments about taking his life and speaking different than usual?! Then having to see him with a 9mm . . . how was I to know one was in the chamber, hot and loaded, ready to fire?!"

To others, I wanted to shout: "You don't get to do this! You don't get to be absent from my life this many years then come back in and tell me what I can and cannot do, or even what calls I can't and can go on! You don't get to do that!"

I could not respond that way. I wanted to say what was floating around in my mind, but I'm a firefighter chaplain . . . to me we aren't allowed to snap. I love being a chaplain, but I do not always like it, because of things like this.

People were saying I shouldn't have lied to Mama, but I did not lie! I told her what she needed to know. I didn't even tell some of my sisters and brothers because I couldn't break the code of conduct or confidentiality. I didn't tell my own blood about the call because I was being a firefighter chaplain. I was also trying to protect them from the pain I had experienced.

And I was also still doing my job. I knew on that day tensions were very high. I knew that if something had happened to me, this would be a very different story. But I was trying to save a life. Many of the officers on scene that day have children, kids I consider my little brothers and sisters and nieces and nephews. And when family is in trouble, you protect your own.

I have brothers and sisters, some in my family and many outside the family. We are very close. If I had called right away and told them what had happened, there would have been a mob. My job as a firefighter chaplain is to handle things but also help keep peace. When I came out of the house that day in 2021, I even said, "Just . . . just don't hurt him."

People think my job is desk work, or people try to keep me from responding to calls. But I answer to one person and one person only, and that is the Lord our God! Now, I know whenever I become active again, there will be a chain of command I will follow to the best of my abilities. But I did not go into that call alone. Not in the way y'all think. I went up there with the Spirit of the Lord upon me, because that's the only way I can explain why and how I made it out of that house.

Luke 10:25-37 says,

> *Just then an expert in the law stood up to test Him, saying, "Teacher, what must I do to inherit eternal life?"*
>
> *"What is written in the law?" He asked him. "How do you read it?"*
>
> *He answered: Love the Lord your God with all your heart, with all your soul, with all your strength, and with all your mind; and your neighbor as yourself.*
>
> *"You've answered correctly," He told him. "Do this and you will live."*
>
> *But wanting to justify himself, he asked Jesus, "And who is my neighbor?"*
>
> *Jesus took up the question and said: "A man was going down from Jerusalem to Jericho and fell into the hands of robbers. They stripped him, beat him up, and fled, leaving him half dead. A priest happened to be going down that road. When he saw him, he passed by on the other side. In the same way, a Levite, when he arrived at the place and saw him, passed by on the other side. But a Samaritan on his journey came up to him, and when he saw the man, he had compassion. He went over to him and bandaged his wounds, pouring on olive oil and wine. Then he put him on his own animal, brought him to an inn, and took care of him. The next day he took out two denarii, gave them to the innkeeper, and said, 'Take care of him. When I come back, I will reimburse you for whatever extra you spend.' Which of these three do you think proved to be a neighbor to the man who fell into the hands of the robbers?"*
>
> *"The one who showed mercy to him," he said.*
>
> *Then Jesus told him, "Go and do the same."*

There are times we tend to be a Hollywood Christian, even when we do not mean to. A Hollywood Christian is someone who wears the cross around their neck and goes to church when they feel like it. A Hollywood Christian picks and chooses what brand of people they want to share the Gospel to or who they want to help.

As a fire chaplain and a straight-up Christian, I say we cannot pick and choose our neighbors. If you see someone struggling, then help them. It may not be in a big way. It may just be, "Hey, can I mow your yard for free. Or can I take the trash out to the road." Or it might be helping a stranger when they slip and fall. You provide what you know in first aid, bandage their wounds, and stay with them until medics arrive.

Or it might be talking someone down from killing themselves, or removing a gun from the person's hand.

It is something to think about as you read that Scripture. Read it again. Which one are you?

Yes, what I did was dangerous, but it is not only my job as a firefighter chaplain to help someone but also to help them as a Christian. Even if I was not a firefighter chaplain. But I know where my heart is with God, and you may not understand this when I say it, but I was called by God to be a firefighter chaplain. I was ordained in a building that people think is just a church. I was prayed over. I made rank as a fire chaplain and was called to be a firefighter chaplain, and I am not just going to half-do my job. If I half-do that, then I refuse to call myself a Christian.

But you may only want me to half-do my job or just hang around in a safe-zone cage. But respectfully, I do not answer to anyone except the Lord our God! I am called by God to serve Him! And I promise you, whenever I am called to a scene or lead, or told to go by the Holy Spirit, whatever actions I need to perform or sacrifices I need to make to get the job done, or whatever message I am told to give to people about our Lord and Savior Jesus Christ, I am going to do it!

Even if it means going to an unknown scene and being unable to see the spiritual flames of what is going on. I might see or feel little red flares telling me something's not right. I walked up there on scene, but spiritually speaking, I rode on the wings of an eagle.

Of the servant of the Lord, David, who spoke the words of this song to the Lord on the day the Lord rescued him from the hand of all his enemies and from the hand of Saul, he said in Psalms 18:1-3:

> *I love You, LORD, my strength.*
> *The LORD is my rock,*
> *my fortress, and my deliverer,*
> *my God, my mountain where I seek refuge,*
> *my shield and the horn of my salvation,*
> *my stronghold.*
> *I called to the LORD, who is worthy of praise,*
> *and I was saved from my enemies.*

I was safe! Even if I did not know it or it seemed like my time on Earth was about to expire.

Gentle Giant is not my enemy, he is my friend and buddy. I mean, who else am I going to watch reruns of *In the Heat of the Night* with? The night after I received the award, I spoke to Gentle Giant. (And I know I ignored orders, but sometimes doing the right thing is not always the easiest. "It's better to ask for forgiveness than permission.") I did not tell him about the award, but I did ask him a question. I asked if he would please come to my book event the following Saturday, October 15th, at church.

He said, "I promise I will be there."

DARK TIDINGS

That night, after speaking with Gentle Giant, Mama and I went to a prayer meeting at church. Some people who attend Flint Hill Baptist Church heard about the award and wanted to speak with me. I was a little embarrassed when Mama mentioned the details of the award and why I received it. I spoke with a lot of people who gave me their words, advice, and guidance. Former US Marine Chris McConnell (who lets me call him by his call sign, Devil Dog, since I had a hard time remembering his name when we first met) and I spoke about a lot of stuff at church that night and later on the phone, and he has been a huge help for me. When we got home, our whole front porch was covered with boxes. I said, "What in the world!" They were the author copies of my first book! I had to store them in the living room until the event next Saturday.

On Sunday October 9th, 2022, there was a social music event at church. My brother and I rode there a little early to help set up. Mama planned to come later. All that day, I had a weird feeling as though something was going to happen. Now, I am not one of those people that can tell the future. Only God can do that. But I sense things. I can feel when a storm is coming, and I will say it is going to be a great storm. People will look at me like, "Chaplain Cheese! It is a beautiful day outside!" Then later, when thunder rumbles and lighting flashes across the sky, they wonder how I knew. It is a gift I am told I have. But this was no storm feeling. At first, I thought I was just nervous about the book launch that coming Saturday because we had a lot more to get done.

I would soon realize this feeling I had was not really a feeling. It was God. It was the same kind of pressure I felt in the hallway that day in November 2021, a protective embrace of love that could only be given by Jesus Christ Himself. Only this time while holding me, the statement was different: "Cheese, My child! I love you, My child. But in a few hours, your life is going to change. It will be dark, and it will be smoky, but fear not, My child, for I am with you!"

If you did not read *Cheezey* or if we have never met, I do what are called "check-ins" on Wednesdays, Fridays, and Sundays. I start with the first name in my contact list and go all the way to the last name. I simply say, "I pray all is well." Often people text me back right then or they may call me the next day, or say I need you, or just say thanks.

During my check-ins this particular Sunday, I was on the phone with Justin Rummage. My pastor asked, "Hey Cheese! Who are you talking to?" I found that odd and thought, *Do I ask who you are talking to?* But I said, "Hey, pastor. I am doing a check-in call. It is one of my Rummage family." He just said, "Okay." Some people were acting weird.

I had just met one of the youth member's friends that night, Jasmine Lee. Jasmine and I have become good friends, and she is one of many I check in and pray with. Whenever I check in with her, I always make sure she is good and try to be there just to listen or let her vent, or give her advice and encourage her. She has one of the biggest hearts. That day, even though she had never met me before, she was very respectful and kind. I was talking with Jasmine when Mama came in, and she had this look on her face. I thought, *I done did something.* I said to Jasmine, "Please excuse me, my mama has that mama look."

As I walked toward her, I could tell she had been crying. Our cousin Tim McCorkle was beside her and I asked what was going on. Tim said, "We are good cousin," while Mama said, "It's your cake!" (We were planning to have cakes at the book event.) When I asked what was wrong with the cakes, she said, "They just wanted to make sure about the names." So I just went off to eat something. But she was hiding the truth of what was actually wrong.

I am cheezey, but I don't really do crowds. I will hang out and go to fires and stuff, but when a whole bunch of people are just standing around talking, I would rather be outside somewhere. I went through the parking lot into the kitchen and saw there were a lot of dishes from the potluck. Whenever I go on mission trips, I would help with some of the clean up after meals, so I started washing away.

I saw Devil Dog and my brother Andrew running back and forth. I did not know of the events that had happened back in Pineville. I also did not know what message of burden Mama was carrying.

So as I washed the dishes, I heard the Undertaker song (or we Southerners know as Johnny Cash's "Ain't No Grave"). At first, I looked out the fire escape exit thinking, *Okay, so where's Taker?* Then I realized it was the guest singers. Then a song started playing with a fast beat, and I started breakdancing with a dish towel like someone was dancing to "Living on a Prayer!"

One of the youths texted me asking where I was. I texted him, "Look up." He was sitting beside Jasmine, and they both started falling out laughing, with Jasmine covering her face with her hands! Only way I can translate that is "OMG, he is insane!" Another youth ran inside and said Tim told him to check on me. He asked what I was doing. I was like, "You know, I just got the Holy Spirit in me or something."

But when it was time to go, Mama shared her message of burden, the one she had hidden from me.

Back in Pineville, Gentle Giant again tried to take his life with a gun. By the grace of God, he was unsuccessful, but was still fighting for his life.

I tried to keep my emotions in check. At that moment, I was in a very dark place. I was still cheezey, but it was dark. Mama wanted us to talk to Pastor Wayne, but I said I was good and just wanted to walk around. As I tried to get my mints out of the pack, I am walking, thinking, *Okay, I got to do this. I got to notify Gentle Giant's family. I got to do this, and I got to do that* . . . then my human side came out and I lost it!

Chris came out of the church, and I said, "Devil Dog! People call me a hero! I'm not no hero! I told y'all I don't deserve the award, just take back the award! He has got more to do! He has got more to do! Why!? Why?! Why?! God, Jesus!"

Being a Marine, Devil Dog could relate to my pain. Chris reminded me that I did save Gentle Giant's life, and I was a hero. I saved his life for a whole year.

But in my mind, I saved his life for a whole year just so he could still pull the trigger. Getting an award is a huge honor, but when Gentle Giant pulled the trigger on himself, it did not really mesh with me. In a way, I felt I had failed him. Because as a fire chaplain, not only are you there to pray, but you are also there to give counsel and give help.

I had a lot of what ifs running through my mind. What if I had requested all firearms be taken away? What if I had reached out to counselors to say this guy needed help? What if I disobeyed orders and still had one-on-one visits? What if I had called him that day to remind him of his promise to come to my event next Saturday? What if I had ridden with Mama instead of Andrew? The list goes on.

We left the church and rode around a little bit. I was already thinking the worst. In the back of my mind, I was saying, *Okay the book event is off. It is time to plan for a funeral.*

Mama told me Jimmy Beasley, my friend and mentor, was waiting on my call, but all I could do was text him saying "NOOOOOO!!!!!"

I needed to check in with Gentle Giant's family. They said he was in the ICU and fighting for his life. Van Phillips told me it was not my fault. But right then, I was still in the "what if" mode. And in my mind, I thought, *Yeah, it was . . .*

I was told not to come to the hospital yet because there was nothing that could be done. So Mama and I went home. I took a shower and stayed in for what seemed forever, just letting my emotions flow. I called Jimmy, and he knew how I felt because of his own journey. I spoke with Andrew and Mama. Even Chris and some others called to check on me.

Some people were trying to make me feel better by telling me that any caliber higher and a person dies right then and there. I guess their intentions were good, but it was not what I needed to hear. I just wanted to tell them to shut up.

The next day would be a lot to take in, but here on this night, I did not care, I had to do something. Some of my fellow firefighters were going to follow procedure and come to collect me so I could go collect family. I had millions of things going through my head how I would react toward them, but Mama reassured me.

If I had been located and told that my assistance was much needed for a call, when I would have been filled in and updated about the patient and the events that had unfolded . . . what would my reaction have been? I would like to say I would have been professional. I mean, we all would like to say that, that we would have a Christian mind and attitude. But honestly, I cannot answer truthfully because I just do not know.

I have always heard that when it is your first—first dead victim, first bad call, first suicide, first fire, first OD—of course, it affects you, but once you get through your first, you're good. I do not know if I fully agree with that. But for this call, I knew what I needed. I needed my questions answered. And other than God, the one who had them was Chris.

So, I called Devil Dog, and we talked the night away. I had so many questions. On that night in November 2021, why didn't the gun go off? Why didn't God take me then or both of us then? Why didn't everything just get better for Gentle Giant?

Could I return my award? Right then, I would have just given it away. But I did not. Chris's advice really helped me and pointed me to Scripture, like John 14:1-6 and Philippians 4:13. He reminded me that I could not save everyone. I knew that, but I was still going on what ifs.

Looking back, this reminds me of a song called "A Soldier's Memoir" by Joe Bachman. I do not have survivors' guilt, nor do I have PTSD (anyone that says otherwise really does not know me at all), but I can see where people who do have it come from.

THE EFFECTS AND DANGERS OF SUICIDE

To my readers, whether we know each other or not, let me speak to you. Here on scene today, for whatever reason, you yourself may be in a dark place right now. As gently as I can, I just want a few minutes of your time. Wait, do not go, please. It is okay. I am not going to be one of those people who say I know where you're coming from, because I do not. Yes, those events in 2021 and 2022 affected me, but it was by the grace of God and the love of Jesus Christ and so many people that have supported me that I am able to hold the line and keep moving forward.

Even if I know you, I know nothing about what you're carrying inside. If you would let me, I would like to try to help you lift some of these burdens off you by telling you about Jesus Christ.

I am going to use firefighting examples. Sometimes when you see firefighters, we are carrying all this fancy equipment, one of the biggest among them is a Halligan bar. You can do a lot with just a Halligan bar. But the biggest tool many people carry (and I am not just talking about firefighters) is our faith. Not just our faith, but our faith in Jesus Christ! Can I please get an Amen?!

Paul says in 2 Corinthians 5:6-10,

> So, we are always confident and know that while we are at home in the body we are away from the Lord. For we walk by faith, not by sight, and we are confident and satisfied to be out of the body and at home with the Lord. Therefore, whether we are at home or away, we make it our aim to be

pleasing to Him. For we must all appear before the tribunal
of Christ, so that each may be repaid for what he has done
in the body, whether good or worthless.

We are not perfect, and we are not going to be perfect. Our faith is what holds us together. Whatever we face, our faith in Christ Jesus will get us through it until we go home and will be in front of the Lord. God knows we are not perfect. He does not except us to go to bed every night and have all A's. He knows how sinful this world is, but He took the punishment of our sins and bore them on Himself.

Psalms 34:18-19 says,

The LORD is near the brokenhearted;
He saves those crushed in spirit.
Many adversities come to the one who is righteous,
but the LORD delivers him from them all.

God knows what is up ahead before we do! The events I spoke about, no, I never saw God, but I did feel Him! He knew on October 9th, 2022, thoughts were going through a person's mind. He was with that person, but He was also with me and many others like my mama who had to carry that horrible message to me. He knows our thoughts, our hearts, and our minds. Even though we may have impure thoughts sometimes or even speak negatively under our breaths about someone, He already knew what was going to be in our minds or come out of our mouths. But guess what, He still loves us!

Psalms 55:22 says,

Cast your burden on the LORD,
and He will sustain you;
He will never allow the righteous to be shaken.

Reader, are you still with me? What burdens are you carrying, bud? What has happened that has made you feel that you no longer deserve to live? Look whatever it is, killing yourself is not the way to handle it. Jesus Christ, who is also God in human form—Yes, God! The one who created the Heavens and the earth—is wanting you to cast anything that is making you feel ill toward yourself or life onto Him! Trust me, He can handle it. I mean, if you see just what He has done in Matthew, Mark, Luke, and John, I mean, bud . . . He took our sins and paid our price with His own blood.

Think of a number right now, please. Now times that by ten. That is how much you mean to Jesus Christ! That is how much He loves you!

Paul says in Romans 8:38-39,

> *For I am persuaded that not even death or life,*
> *angels or rulers,*
> *things present or things to come, hostile powers,*
> *height or depth, or any other created thing*
> *will have the power to separate us*
> *from the love of God that is in Christ Jesus our Lord!*

My friend! Sweet, sweet victory! It can all be found in Jesus Christ! Whatever sins you have done, whatever heavy cross of burdens you're carrying, let it go! Because nothing can separate us from Jesus Christ!

When Jesus was agonizing on the Cross, there were two thieves being crucified next to Him. One thief said to Jesus, "If You are truly The Christ, then get us down from here." But the other thief rebuked him and said, "Jesus, remember me when You come into Your kingdom." If you are familiar with the Bible, what did Jesus say to the thief who believed in Him? If you do not know it, I got you. He said, "I tell you the truth! Today, you will be with me in paradise!"

Now people often say you have to be baptized to go to Heaven, or if you are not baptized you are not a Christian. Where does it say that in Luke or any part of the Bible? It never says anything about the thief being baptized (Luke 23:32-43). This thief had done evil deeds and now he was getting paid back, but in his last few moments, rather than give insults like the other thief, he used his few moments to say to God, "Save me! I am sorry for what I did. Do not make me suffer any more then I have to!"

Jesus never brought up any of his past falls, all He saw was the man and his heart and gave him forgiveness right there on the Cross. Before this, when Jesus was being crucified by the Roman soldiers, what did He say? He said, "Forgive them Father! For they know not what they do."

If the God of the universe, who is also Jesus Christ in human form, can forgive the men who nailed His hands and feet to the Cross and also forgive a thief for his trespasses, then how can you not find it in your heart to forgive not only yourself but others that have hurt you?

Isaiah 40:28-31 says,

> *Do you not know?*
> *Have you not heard?*
> *Yahweh is the everlasting God,*
> *the Creator of the whole earth.*
> *He never grows faint or weary;*
> *there is no limit to His understanding.*
> *He gives strength to the weary*
> *and strengthens the powerless.*
> *Youths may faint and grow weary,*
> *and young men stumble and fall,*
> *but those who trust in the LORD*
> *will renew their strength;*
> *they will soar on wings like eagles;*
> *they will run and not grow weary;*
> *they will walk and not faint.*

Reader, fear not, for the God of the whole universe is with you!

Isaiah 41:10-13 says,

> Do not fear, for I am with you;
> do not be afraid, for I am your God.
> I will strengthen you; I will help you;
> I will hold on to you with My righteous right hand.
> Be sure that all who are enraged against you
> will be ashamed and disgraced;
> those who contend with you
> will become as nothing and will perish.
> You will look for those who contend with you,
> but you will not find them.
> Those who war against you
> will become absolutely nothing.
> For I, Yahweh your God,
> hold your right hand
> and say to you: Do not fear,
> I will help you.

I have never been in a full-on burning building, but I have been on some calls that made my stomach twist. But in those times, there was no need to fear, even though the world seemed like it was crashing down. For God was among the scene.

Just like God helped me, He will help you. He will strengthen you and give you the ability to get out of this dark hole you are in. And when the day is over, you will have victory through Jesus Christ! Because God has got your 6 (that means back)!

Let us talk about Lazarus and look in the Gospel of John. (By the way John is one of my favorite scriptures in the Bible, in case you are wondering.)

John 11:17-44 says,

> When Jesus arrived, He found that Lazarus had already been in the tomb four days. Bethany was near Jerusalem (about two miles away). Many of the Jews had come to Martha and Mary to comfort them about their brother. As soon as Martha heard that Jesus was coming, she went to meet Him. But Mary remained seated in the house.
>
> Then Martha said to Jesus, "Lord, if You had been here, my brother would not have died. Yet even now I know that whatever You ask from God, God will give You."
>
> "Your brother will rise again," Jesus told her.
>
> Martha said, "I know that he will rise again in the resurrection at the last day."
>
> Jesus said to her, "I am the resurrection and the life. The one who believes in Me, even if he dies, will live. Everyone who lives and believes in Me will never die—ever. Do you believe this?"
>
> "Yes, Lord," she told Him, "I believe You are the Messiah, the Son of God, who comes into the world."
>
> Having said this, she went back and called her sister Mary, saying in private, "The Teacher is here and is calling for you."
>
> As soon as she heard this, she got up quickly and went to Him.
>
> Jesus had not yet come into the village but was still in the place where Martha had met Him. The Jews who were with her in the house consoling her saw that Mary got up quickly and went out. So, they followed her, supposing that she was going to the tomb to cry there.
>
> When Mary came to where Jesus was and saw Him, she fell

at His feet and told Him, "Lord, if You had been here, my brother would not have died!"

When Jesus saw her crying, and the Jews who had come with her crying, He was angry in His spirit and deeply moved. "Where have you put him?" He asked.

"Lord," they told Him, "come and see."

Jesus wept.

So the Jews said, "See how He loved him!" But some of them said, "Couldn't He who opened the blind man's eyes also have kept this man from dying?"

Then Jesus, angry in Himself again, came to the tomb. It was a cave, and a stone was lying against it. "Remove the stone," Jesus said.

Martha, the dead man's sister, told Him, "Lord, he's already decaying. It's been four days."

Jesus said to her, "Didn't I tell you that if you believed you would see the glory of God?"

So they removed the stone. Then Jesus raised His eyes and said, "Father, I thank You that You heard Me. I know that You always hear Me, but because of the crowd standing here I said this, so they may believe You sent Me."

After He said this, He shouted with a loud voice, "Lazarus, come out!" The dead man came out bound hand and foot with linen strips and with his face wrapped in a cloth. Jesus said to them, "Loose him and let him go."

Lazarus had been dead for four days, and of course, this was part of God's plan. Listen, I do not care what sickness you have, last time I checked, God is the one who receives and gives life.

Can I please get an Amen!?

There is a lot of Scripture to cover here, but I really want to get to the core of this. Some people may think that a man who was dead for four days walking out of the grave is core. And that is! But this part is also the core!

> Jesus said to her, "I am the resurrection and the life. The one who believes in Me, even if he dies, will live. Everyone who lives and believes in Me will never die—ever. Do you believe this?"

Jesus can and will lift up people from the dead! This man was dead for four days and walked out of the tomb after Jesus called him. Listen, and I will speak carefully because I have got to say this in an easy way. First you may say, "But Chaplain Cheese, that man did not shoot himself in the head. That man did not jump off a bridge." But that is missing the point! It did not matter if the man had COVID, Stage 4 cancer, or pulled a gun on himself. The point is Jesus brought him back!

I care about you! Even if we have never crossed paths, I do care about you. But I do not care how you're planning this, because if you pull the trigger or jump off a roof, people can give all sorts of numbers of how likely you'll survive. But the Lord has the final say if you die or if you are given another chance at life.

Now many people believe that if you commit suicide you are going to hell. I do not necessarily believe that. I believe that there are God-fearing Christians out there, and often they get stressed out (like we all do). They get fed a bunch of lies, and instead of going to someone or going to God, they take their life. Some do not succeed, but some do. For the ones that do not come back from it, I truly believe if they sincerely gave their heart to Jesus Christ, they will be in Heaven. Now, God may have a talk with them, but wholeheartedly, I believe that they will go to Heaven.

Suicide is a very dangerous, selfish thing! It is the Devil's favorite toy! But it's not a toy for you. Suicide affects everyone! Now listen, I do honestly care about you, and I said this because I love you as a sibling, friend, Christian, and firefighter chaplain. The selfish decision you're thinking about making right now will not only affect you for the rest of your life and beyond, but it will also affect the people you know and love, as well as your community.

Bang! You shoot and kill yourself. Then it takes people to dark places saying: How did you get to this point of your life without telling me? How could you do this to us? How could you kill yourself and let me pick up the pieces? I should have known you had this going on! Why was I not aware of whatever you were carrying? I cannot live without you, so just like you hurt your family and friends, I am going to hurt my family and friends so I can come to see you. Could I have done more?

All suicide does is bring more pain to others. You kill yourself because you are in pain, then someone else kills themselves because they are in pain. It goes on and on and on, until there is no more life on this earth or in your family of friends.

Reader, I am not trying to hurt you. I am trying to help you! To help you see how your decision not only affects your life but also others and God. Yes, God! You're robbing others of more time they could have had with you, and you're slapping God in the face for the blessings and future He had for you down here. You're saying, "Okay God, I am going to be the one that says when I depart from this earth." But that is not what God wants for you.

God loves you! He has a message just for you that He has laid upon my heart to tell you today: My child, your life is not broken, your life is beautiful. Deep in the hearts of many, there is an emptiness. An emptiness that they believe can be cured by such false things of this dark, desperate, angry, frightening, cruel world, like drugs, alcohol, pornography, or even death by whatever means. None of that can ever fill that emptiness in your heart that you have. Listen to me please, God's love is real! He died for you and for me and the world.

Jesus says in John 3:16-18,

> *For God loved the world in this way: He gave His One and Only Son, so that everyone who believes in Him will not perish but have eternal life. For God did not send His Son into the world that He might condemn the world, but that the world might be saved through Him. Anyone who believes in Him is not condemned, but anyone who does not believe is already condemned, because he has not believed in the name of the One and Only Son of God.*

You may say, "Chaplain Cheese, I got Buddha." But no earthly religion can save you! Again, people get religion and Christianity mixed up. "Religion is the following of doctrine or beliefs and traditions in allegiance to please or to be in a right relationship with God. Christianity is a religion, but we understand that it first must be rooted in a personal relationship with God and Jesus Christ. Without that relationship, there can be no salvation; it is only empty religion."

God's love is beyond real! And here today, if you open up your heart to God, He will come in and fill that emptiness with His love, mercy, hope and more! That is the message!

In Revelation 3:20 Jesus says,

> *Listen! I stand at the door and knock. If anyone hears My voice and opens the door, I will come in to him and have dinner with him, and he with Me.*

Here on scene, you might not even be a Christian, or you may have placed your faith in Jesus Christ when you were very young, but it is only here at this moment that you fully understand it all. If that is you right here today, I would like to lead you in a prayer.

> *Dear Lord Jesus, here this day, I admit to you that I am a sinner. I believe that God raised You from the dead. I ask You right here today to forgive me of my sins. And also, here today I confess You as my Lord and Savior. Come into my heart. Be my Lord and Savior. In Jesus' name I pray. Amen.*

If you have just prayed this prayer and you meant it, I want you to know that all of Heaven is rejoicing! Jesus is starting to prepare you a room in Heaven today, right here, right now! You have just taken hold of the defining "wave prayer" moment in your life that can only be found through the blood of Jesus Christ. You have just embraced the biggest decision of your life, and you have been redeemed!

I encourage you to tell people about what you have done here today! Tell them your story and also to study the Bible. If you do not have a Bible, I encourage you to go and buy one. Three versions I recommend are the HCSB (Christian Holman Standard Bible), King James Study Bible, or the ESV Study Bible. If you are not part of a church family, I encourage you to pray that God will lead you to one where you can connect with Him. I am a part of Flint Hill Baptist Church, and if you are in the Pineville area, I'd recommend you check them out.

I also encourage you to get baptized. It does not stop every sin coming your way, but when we get baptized:

1. It says, "Jesus, I want You to know and see that I am really all in for You."
2. It symbolizes us being washed of our sins. It symbolizes what God has done in our hearts already.
3. Our old selves die, and we identify with Christ in raising to walk a new life and being reborn.

Reader, if you are having thoughts of suicide right now or you struggle with PTSD, there is help for you out there. If you are having these thoughts, I need you to place a bookmark right here, pick up the phone, and dial 911. You do not have to be ashamed. You need help, and right now you are starting the first stage of it. If you would like your loved ones to be notified, please tell the dispatcher, but do not hang up.

Before we move on, let us pray:

Dear Lord Jesus, I ask that You be with this reader here today. Lord Jesus, we ask that You will be with their heart and mind and we ask that You will allow them Your peace, hope, and love. Lord Jesus, if a decision was made in You today, we jump for joy together. We ask that You will allow them to be able to tell their story to others today. And Lord Jesus, if they are in a dark place today, we ask that You set them free from this place and, if needed, allow my fellow brothers and sisters to get to their need quickly. We ask that You forgive us of our sins. In Jesus' name, we pray. Amen.

A LETTER TO A GENTLE GIANT

Dear Gentle Giant,

This was God putting this on my heart. I know we've been through a lot together. Though we have been through rough waters, we have also been through calm seas. Every time I came in the house, I would say hey to you, and before I would sit down, you would say, "Aren't you going to get your bat to hold." Then one day, you told me to take it. I still have it. Every time I watch the movie *A Few Good Men*, I hold it close to me. Thanks again for it!

I miss hanging out and the laughs we had. People want to talk about the heroic actions that were performed that day, but they do not know the actions that you have performed. Matthew 25:35-36 says,

> *For I was hungry*
> *and you gave Me something to eat;*
> *I was thirsty*
> *and you gave Me something to drink;*
> *I was a stranger and you took Me in;*
> *I was naked and you clothed Me;*
> *I was sick and you took care of Me;*
> *I was in prison and you visited Me.*

When I used to work for you, mowing your yard, you would run down to the dive in and grab us a couple of burgers to eat. When it looked like I needed a fresh bottle of water, you gave me something to drink. Though we knew each other, we didn't know each other well, but you still took me in as a friend, lawn-care guy, and also as a son.

When I was dealing with sickness, you checked in on me and encouraged me to get better. When I had foot surgery to get a bunion removed, I felt like I was in prison because for a few days after surgery I could not walk or go anywhere, but you came and visited me. When it came to my family, you made sure I was respectful and still held tight to the Words of Jesus Christ.

So, no sir, I am not a hero. You were the hero, and still are. Because even through your struggles, you still managed to be a servant of Jesus Christ in your own way. I never got a chance to tell you, but I think it is time for you to hear it from me: Gentle Giant, I had already forgiven you! Most people might have their comments to say, but our only judge is Jesus Christ Himself, and He already stood and died for us.

I still look to you as my friend. Bud, I cannot tell you when I will be able to come up there and do one-on-one visits again. If it were up to me, I would come and see you, but for reasons that will not be mentioned, I am unable. But I do promise you one day we will be able to hang out again and have our laughs and stories, either here on Earth or up above when God calls us home—on His time, not ours!

You may not remember this, but I told you a long time ago that God is going to use your story to help someone with theirs. You may say your story is old and dark. But I say your story is fresh, new, and redeemable! Not because of the works you do, but because of the love and hope of Jesus Christ that is around you and also in the core of your heart.

If you have not heard anything else I have said, then please now, hear me, and rejoice! For the Lord our God has given not only you a blessing, but your entire family. There is still work that needs to be done and your story is far from over. So, rise up and take hold because you are going to be able to use your story and personal testimony to help bring someone to Jesus Christ.

You will be able to sing the songs we used to sing together in your living room, like "Amazing Grace,"

I once was lost, but now I am found, was blind but now I see.

I look forward to the day you stand in front of a church pulpit and tell your story. I love you Gentle Giant.

MINISTERING IN UNCHARTED WATERS

The events of October 9th, 2022, did not only affect me but many other people. To say I had a good night's sleep or any sleep at all that night would just be me trying to make people feel better. I had tons of text messages and missed calls from friends and family and fellow first responders, along with my own chaplain.

I came out of my room and the first thing I asked Mama was, "Have you heard anything on Gentle Giant's condition?" She told me he was stable, but I needed to call the family, then it was time to rub some dirt on my heart and go to work. Not to cut grass! But to be a firefighter chaplain among my community. I got dressed quickly and grabbed my Bible. I did not even bother to shower, and I cannot remember if I walked or ran, but somehow, I was at the door of my first stop. Among my stops were the Helms. I sat down with Mrs. Donna, talking and praying with her. But instead of me being there for them, Mrs. Donna was there for me.

After leaving, TJ called me. I thought he was at the airport ready to go on a mission trip, but to my surprise, TJ was in Pineville on duty and wanted to go to lunch with me. We went to the dive in. Most people from Pineville were there, many reaching out to me. Even one of my Pineville sisters stopped her job and took the time to tell me new information: there was brain activity. I just sat there with TJ, thinking, *What is it You want from me, Lord?! What is your plan for all of this?*

TJ and I spent some time praying and talking, giving me additional details he heard about the recent event, then he took me home. I had texted Gentle Giant's family and was told I was needed, but to come that evening to the hospital. I took a shower, got dressed, and went outside where my friend Marcus had stopped by. He reminded me that I was not the only one struggling, trying to find answers, nor was I the only one who was having to go through this.

I don't remember all the details of all the conversations I had, but I remember the power of prayer, faith, love, and peace in the midst of it. People kept reminding me it was not my fault. Again, you get an award for stopping a man from pulling the trigger on himself a year before, then four or five days later, that same person pulls the trigger again and succeeds. Can anybody explain it to me? Because I do not understand.

Then again, maybe there is no explaining. Maybe we already know the answer. Many times, we think when events like 9/11 or the Boston Bombing happen or a tornado touches down on a small town, we ask, "Where was God?!" And of course, He is always on scene. But free will can be a bad thing, because we misuse it. This may have you asking, "Chaplain Cheese, what are you saying?!"

Before one of these devastating events, in your busy day, would you even think about giving a stranger a hug or helping them out? It might cross your mind, but would you have gone from thinking to physically acting? Would you have gone up to a person you barely know or even a total stranger and say, "Hey, I want to give you a hug because I see you need it, and I also want to remind you that God loves you and it is going to be okay."? What about getting a whole bunch of first responders together and saying, "Hey, let's do a 5k in honor of the fallen men and women. Or a stair climb for fallen police and firefighters!"?

Even though bad things happen, we can still have faith and know that through darkness, light still shines out! Can I please get an Amen?!

Paul says in, 2 Corinthians 4:6,

> For God who said, "Let light shine out of darkness," has shone in our hearts to give the light of the knowledge of God's glory in the face of Jesus Christ.

What Paul is saying here is to give back the knowledge. Remember how you felt when you first became a Christian? Did you run around saying, "I am saved! I am saved!" Did you call up your best friend saying, "Hey, can we meet up? I need to tell you something!" Only to find out she had the same thing to tell you! Telling everyone of the knowledge you received about Jesus Christ is not just knowledge, it is lifesaving knowledge. Can I please get an Amen?

When disasters strike, choices are made, or homes destroyed and families broken, darkness tends to hang around. But when prayers are spoken, scriptures read from the Bible, and the comfort of Jesus Christ is given it makes the days become brighter. It is not going to be a bottle of Jack Daniels. It will not be any kind of drug. It will only be found in the bright hands of Jesus Christ! Can I please get an Amen?!

Later that evening, it was time for me to go to the one place I needed to minister: the hospital where Gentle Giant's family was waiting. When Mama and I walked into the room, I greeted Gentle Giant's family but then went to him. To my surprise, he was somewhat alert, with his eyes wide open. There were a lot of tubes and machines around him. I started off by saying something simple, "I love you," then began to read Scripture. I spoke with his family and prayed for them as well. I was tasked with locating an item for Gentle Giant, and thankfully, I did not have to return to the scene to do so. When it was time to leave, many nurses and doctors greeted me.

On Sunday, I was upset. Monday, I was angry. And Tuesday, I was confused. I kept thinking, *Did this really happen?* I was still receiving many calls, but I was also reaching out to check on people myself. Even though I was able to see Gentle Giant, my heart was still shattered, not only for myself but also for him and his family and friends. The week moved on and I was able to locate the item they asked for. After I went to pick it up, from all places, the Pineville Fire House, I was greeted by many of my fellow brothers who knew of the events and how I was affected. They offered me great advice.

Often, we try to keep things bottled up, but then God intervenes. I will say, He is a loving God! There's no doubt or question about that.

THE RELEASE OF CHEEZEY

Throughout all this, the day of my book release event arrived on the second night of the Pineville Fall Fest, October 15th. I had spoken with my Utah nephew Gavin, who told me he and Aubrey and others wished they could be there to support me. Gavin asked, "Uncle Cheese, when are you coming home? You haven't been here since 2019!" I said, "Bud, you know if I could, I would get you here, but I cannot." I felt something was up. But then again, my mind was in a million places. They didn't know about the other recent events. When it comes to my Utah kids, I try my hardest to keep my firefighting work stuff away from them. I assured him I wanted to make a trip soon.

We had much to do that day. My family and I had arrived at the church early, needing to set up my book display but also to beat the Fall Fest traffic. The plan was for me to stay in the choir room until it was time for the launch of *Cheezey* to start.

People said that I seemed cheezey that day, but looks can be deceiving. In my mind, I was in a dark place. I was thinking about Gentle Giant. See, as a fire chaplain, when one of your people is sick or in the hospital or a crisis has occurred, your duty is to be with them. I was thinking, *Am I right to be here?* I was also worried about how this book would do. Some people saw that I was not myself that day.

Before the service started, my cousin Michael and I were hanging out. Next thing I hear is the door swinging wide open, and Mama said, "Cheese, I'm sorry, but you're in trouble!"

I did not have time to respond because all of a sudden Gavin came flying around the corner along with his sister (my niece), Aubrey. I knew

Ms. Rummage was coming, but I was shocked to see my niece and nephew. I said, "You lied to me!" But I was still laughing and got a big hug from both of them. That is just what I needed to be cheezey again!

The service started and I was advised that when you release a book, you should talk about why you wanted to write it. So after I spoke, while Jimmy was singing, my family and I moved to the fellowship hall. We had a lot of food and two big cakes. So many people came! There were those from Pineville and the Stough Memorial Baptist Church. Some of the James family came, one of my best friend's grandmothers came, and many people from church. As I was signing books, I noticed Jackie Jennings, Mama, my aunt, and some of our Pineville family sitting together with some of our church members telling stories about me. Only the good Lord knows what was said about me!

I was so honored to have some of Gentle Giant's family come. I was able to give them the item they asked for. I introduced Jimmy and his wife to them, and I feel like much stress was lifted off that family.

One of my friends was unable to be there because she had planned a mountain trip. However, her parents were there. I guess you could say I am the adopted son in this family. They have two daughters who are both my sisters, but their youngest daughter, who I have a very close relationship with, had no idea of what had been happening. Well, Mama had told her dad everything about past events and the award. Her dad is also an EMT. From across the room, he stared me down then came over and said, "Son, we need to have a talk . . . right now."

At first, I was thinking, *Are we really going to do this right here in front of everybody?* But I did need a break from sitting and there was a pause in the line for signing, so we went out into the hallway and he said, "You have got to tell her. Do you understand me?" He was not being mean or anything. I understand his view completely, which to me can only be said like this: "If you love my daughter, who is also your sister, the way you say you do, and you care about her the way you say you do, then you will tell her everything and leave nothing out. You will stop keeping and hiding this from her."

I had many things going through my head, but the biggest thing was, *This is going to break her heart.* And I was going to be the one to do it. But I also knew if she heard it from someone else, it would be ten times worse. One thing me and this sister of mine have is trust. Though my sisters and I might be close, we each have a different style. This sister's style has always been to use her voice before anything. If she needs to, she raises her voice and uses her stare! But her voice is gentle. And yeah, times when I was younger, I was a handful. But it was by the grace of God that I had my mama and people like my sisters to be there for me.

As a firefighter chaplain, I have a rule and it is not only my rule, but also the rule of chaplaincy. When handling a call, you do not speak of it to anyone unless the person's life is in danger or someone else's life is in danger. And I have followed that code of conduct. I try very hard to live by that code, which many times is extremely hard and painful, but I still manage to follow it. I kept this locked down from family and friends. The only people that knew of the events were the people that were on Central or on scene.

Now I mentioned earlier that when we try to keep things bottled up, God intervenes, well this was His way of doing it. I guess God saw how much of a heavy burden I was carrying around and said, "Okay Cheese, it's time for you to be free of it."

Her dad finally said, "This is how we will do this. She comes home to pick her dog up at our house tomorrow afternoon. You have until she pulls in my driveway to tell her. If she pulls in our driveway tomorrow afternoon and you have not told her, she is going to hear it from me! And you know what is going to happen then."

All is well with my sister and me. Though many people found out through many different ways and people and gave me their two cents on it, I can honestly say this was the first time I did not feel there was a tone or tension of judgment.

Despite this talking to, the release of *Cheezey* was awesome. We sold around one hundred and fifty books and almost half of the shirts we had made. After the event, people were coming to the house and reaching out for more! Even though I have my first book out, I am still the same Cheese . . . but even cheezier!

As I was working on this book, I was having to gather my thoughts and relive some of the events. Well, I cannot keep this in anymore. Many people used to say, "Watch your 6," or "The person that I know and the person you know are different." I used to ask what that meant, and no one would ever tell me. Most people know that if you're trying to teach me something, you cannot just give me step one and two and expect me to figure out three, four, and five.

But I guess I *can* do that. I figured out the next steps and when the situation arose, I did not hesitate to do what needed to be done! I do not blame anybody, nor am I trying to hurt anybody! Honestly, I was frustrated mostly with myself for not understanding. But looking back, God had me there for a reason.

I honestly get sick and tired of all the talking: "It's not your job!" Or "You cannot do that anymore!" Or "You will not do that anymore."

You're right, I cannot do it. But God can, has, and will do it! I am not saying I am God. What I am saying is what Jesus says in Matthew 19:26,

> But Jesus Looked at them and said. "With men this is impossible, But with God all things are possible."

God gave me the strength and wisdom to get the job done. And not only this job but other jobs that have come along and will continue to come along!

I noticed a lot of people had mixed feelings about what happened. But who are you really upset with? Looking at all of it now, were you mad at yourself for not telling me the rest of the steps? Or were you mad at me for not understanding? Or both?

Do you ever think of what could have happened if I had not been there that day? Do you ever think what could have happened if I had fully understood? Would I have been up there in the first place?

Thank God we will never know.

BEYOND CHEEZEY

After *Cheezey*, everything started to settle down. I did make some money, but it is not really about money. If God gives me it, I will put it toward my truck. Sadly, right after I got home from the book event, my bed I had for years finally gave up and broke. So I had to put half the money into a new bed.

After all of the excitement, I was able to settle down. When I wasn't cutting grass or maintaining yards, I was able to do things like go to Asheboro or hang out with my brother-in-law, out shooting or four wheeling. Back home in Pineville, I started hunting more often with my friend Mr. Hopkins. We are as country as cornflakes. I was able to get my first deer last year! I still have my learner's permit, but I was able to get more driving practice in and keep saving for my truck with the money I made selling books and shirts over Thanksgiving and Christmas that year.

Now as I said before, I am just a firefighter chaplain. When I am on a scene and asked to help in a medical way, the first thing I tell people is that I am not an EMT. I have some training, but I am not fully certified. However, I was taught to always have a first aid bag on hand, just in case. It is better to have a little of something than have nothing.

One day, a week before Christmas, Mama and I were running some errands and were on our way to grab a bite to eat at Park 51. It was raining a little bit, and I noticed a woman bending over but could not really see what was happening. As we were walking into the restaurant, the woman started screaming, "Sir, we need some help!" An elderly woman had slipped and fell on her way out of the hair salon.

I told Mama to grab my bag. As I came over, I said. "I am a firefighter chaplain, but I am not EMT certified." The woman who had asked for help said she did not care and to just help the elderly woman. That annoyed me, but I brushed it off.

I knelt near the victim, and soon a crowd was gathering. I told people if they were not nurses or anything to step away. The less people you have crowding around the better. If too many people are around a victim, they tend to be more frightened. With fewer people, the victim is easier to settle down. I noticed she had a laceration on the left side of her temple, which was bleeding pretty good. I asked if 911 had been called and when it was said that they hadn't, I directed people to alert 911 and let them know a fire chaplain was on scene.

Mama returned with my bag, which had some gauze, bandages, and gloves. I asked the victim if she could tell me her name and if she remembered what happened. She was a little shaken up but still able to answer my questions. She started complaining of neck pain.

The woman that had called me over would not stop screaming and yelling about how we needed to move her to a chair. Mama told her, "Ma'am! My son knows what he is doing. You need to stand back and let him do his job. If he needs us to help, he will let us know."

Here are a couple of things I learned when it comes to a victim of a head injury: Try to keep them as still as possible, do not move them unless there is danger. And if they are complaining of neck pain, do not move them and try to keep them still. If you do not have a neck brace, be the neck brace.

The gentlemen that called 911 said they were asking him questions he did not know. So I took over and had him hold the lady's head. I had finally gotten her to calm down. All seemed quite well until the woman that had called me over started yelling and screaming again.

I finally went into full fire mode. "Step off! Step off, ma'am. You called me over here, and I am doing my job. Right now, you're interfering with this call and upsetting my victim. Either you stand there and keep your mouth shut or you leave. Otherwise, I am going to request Central to send the PD and have them remove you from the scene! Do I make myself clear?!"

Finally, she left. I took over patient care again. Pineville Fire finally arrived with the Rescue 12 (medic truck) and were first on scene. Thankfully, my buddy Greg Clark, who was my Lieutenant and my captain when I was active with Pineville, was on that call. I think he was surprised to see me there. I told him, "Yeah, I know I am not with Pineville no more, but I was requested over here."

He said something like, "Cheese, you're good!" I gave him the information of what happened, and when he was ready to take over patient care, I stepped out of the way. He said I did a good job of securing her head and stopping the bleeding.

How I got the victim calmed down was simple. I told her about Jesus and asked about her faith. She was Christian and had a lot of faith. When the medics arrived, she started getting nervous again, but I assured her she was in good hands.

I began searching for her emergency contact by looking at her last known caller, which was her daughter. I called and after one ring, the daughter picked up. I relayed what had happened, what hospital her mother was going to, and that her car was still on scene. She said that she lives out of town, but she would call her sister in Charlotte, who could be there. I assured her that everything seemed okay and handed the phone to her mama so they could have a good talk.

I helped the medics and Captain Greg get loaded back up. I was told to find a bottle of bleach to pour on the blood on the concrete to kill the germs. I went to the hair salon, and even though I had my badge, they said no. I understood because you can use bleach for good or bad purposes. The workers at Park 51 gave me some and I was able to get the scene cleaned up. After all was done, I went to wash my hands and put my stuff up. Mama asked, "Can we eat now?"

I cannot remember the victim's name, but if you are reading this, I pray all is well and that you were able to have a blessed, happy, and safe Christmas with your family and friends.

RON HEEFNER

After COVID, when Flint Hill started to meet again, I met Ronnie. He was still grieving the loss of his wife, Bobbie. His home was down the street from my uncle's house. Unable to cut the grass, he asked if I could help and would pay me a little. I told him no payment was required and I started working for him. We struck up a friendship.

One thing about Ronnie is that he wanted to serve God! It did not matter what temperature it was outside that day, or where the location was, Ronnie wanted to go serve God and the church. Mr. Ronnie had a lot of health issues, but he did not let that stop him from going places.

On February 1st, 2023, Flint Hill Baptist was having one of our monthly business meetings. I am the lead security over our church security team. After the meeting, Ronnie seemed a little off, but I didn't think much of it because when he sits for a while, it takes him a while to get back to walking and standing. I walked Ronnie out to his car, as usual. It was a God thing on this night.

I usually help him get into the car then go behind it to my mama's car. But on that night, we had Ms. Nancy with us. She had asked us to give her a ride to church, so Mama parked to the left side of the building near the street. I had a feeling something was not right. We decided to follow Ronnie home. While waiting for him to leave, I was on my phone. Suddenly, Mama and Nancy cried out, "He just hit a car! He just backed into Randy's car!"

Immediately, I made my way out of the car but couldn't see Mr. Ronnie or his vehicle. I retrieved my firelight from Mama's car. Then Ronnie's car appeared, and it looked as though he was having a medical emergency. I gave the order for Mr. Ron to stop, saying anything to get his attention. "Fire department! Fire chaplain, stop! Flint Hill security, stop! Ronnie, stop the car, it is me, Cheeseburger!"

He looked at me, his hands shaking, then slumped over the steering wheel. His car was still moving slowly. I believed he was suffering from cardiac arrest or a severe seizure. I ran in my cowboy boots, side by side with the car. When I felt it was safe, I pulled the door open, jumped in the car, and jerked the keys out of the ignition.

Mama said, "I told you to stop him and help him! I did not tell you to jump in his moving car with your feet dangling out!" I thought she was coming with me, but she had run inside the church for more help.

I asked Ronnie if he could hear me and to squeeze my hand if he could. He was unresponsive. In the back of my mind, I was saying, *God, help us! Ronnie, come back to me! Don't go! God, please help us.* I alerted 911. Maybe ten seconds later, Ron became alert and complained of neck and back pain. I got in the back of the car and held his head still until fire and medic arrived.

Many people came running out of the church. Some of them saw me and thought I was the victim. Fire and medic arrived and told the crowd to get back. Mama told me that many of them were telling her to get me out of there because of my seizures (referring to the fire engine and medic lights), but I do not have seizures anymore. I have been on many scenes with flashing lights and they did not phase me. I have not dealt with much vertigo, and if I do, it is just a few minutes. I just rest, then three to five minutes later, I am cheezey.

One of the firefighters pulled me aside. He wanted to know how the car was stopped. When I told him, he responded by saying, "Cheese! Now, I have been in the fire service for a very long time! What fire class did I miss that it said to jump in a moving car to help or save someone?"

I said, "The part where you have to overcome and adapt."

He smiled and said alright. It seemed to me that some of the other officers on scene were trying to blame me for Ronnie's shape. But that same firefighter stood up for me and told them any questions that they needed to ask me, talk to him about it instead.

I was told to find people to help me track down Ronnie's information and call his son Ryan. While waiting for his family to come, we prayed with Mr. Ron and reminded him of God's love and peace. Ronnie was pretty shaken up. His family arrived, but Ronnie did not want to go to the hospital. His family and many church members said he should. Ronnie asked me to come with. So he left for the hospital with his family, and Mama and I followed. I was unable to stay with him because of visiting hours and restrictions.

I was starting to feel the effects of my actions. I mean running, then jumping in a car, and turning your body in different ways does not feel good. Plus running in cowboy boots . . . let's just say, I finally broke that pair in. When I got home that night, I had to clean up my clothes and shower. For whatever reason, most of us had white paint or dust on our hands and clothes. I called our deacon, Mike Culp, and he told me his concerns about my actions. He agreed my actions were justified but said they were also dangerous and life threatening.

Since the events in November 2021, I've heard people say I need to start using my head more or I need to think about how my actions will affect the people around me that I love. Respectfully, I try not to think about it because, for me, it is an excuse not to do the job or it becomes a distraction for you to handle the task at hand. It is just your fear getting in the way! Of course I could stand down and call 911, but any first responder can tell you there is a time limit to help. It's two to three minutes, maybe more if you're lucky. Time is not on the victim's side.

Honestly, a million things are going through my mind. I'll think about how people say things like, "You're autistic, you don't know how to do it," or "You do not know how to even help yourself." But when handling issues or if I am called upon, I try to keep a very clear mind, because if my mind becomes unclear or I focus on those comments, how will I be of any help to a person who needs help? I also have the biggest and ultimate insurance policy that will not expire, and that is found in the blood of Jesus Christ! Can I please get an Amen?!

The next day, I woke up so sore but found the strength through Jesus Christ to move forward. I had many people calling me from church asking Ronnie's status and how I was feeling. Ronnie had returned home in the late morning hours, so Nana dropped me off at his house. Before we spoke of the events from the night before, Ronnie and I prayed together. Then we found ourselves laughing and crying a little.

FOR RONNIE

This past summer, my best friend Ronnie was called home to Heaven. I was one of the few that had the honor and the privilege of speaking at his funeral. This is the sermon I gave (edited for brevity):

The Bible I am reading out of is the HCSB. Our Scripture reading comes from Colossians 3:1-2:

> So if you have been raised with the Messiah, seek what is above, where the Messiah is, seated at the right hand of God. Set your minds on what is above, not on what is on the earth.

We are gathering to celebrate the life of Ronnie Heefner. The Saturday I was notified of Mr. Ron's stroke, I started thinking of verses and songs like John 14:1-6. Now you can ask almost any chaplain, preacher, or minister a good passage for a funeral or for a reminder when it seems it is the end or you're just down in the dumps looking for even the tiniest bit of hope. We will refer you to John 14:1-6. It is more than just a funeral passage. It is more than a reminder, because it is *the* reminder!

In times like these, we should open up God's Word. Jesus is reminding us that He has gone away, then came back, but went away again until either my room is finished or someone else's room is finished. So, when it is all done, He comes back to take either me or them with Him to remain and live in paradise! Can I please get an Amen?!

Many people do not get paradise, but we can rest assured that when God called Mr. Ronnie home, he has been truly called home by not only his but our Lord and Savior Jesus Christ to the streets of glory! Can I please get an Amen?!

I know many of us have questions. Many of us are trying to make sense of it, trying to wrap our heads around the fact that when we last had contact with him, he seemed fine. He was even smiling, having a good time! From the time we left until now, what happened? Can someone please answer that? Because I do not understand! I do not understand!

But it is then at that moment where our Scripture reading comes into play! "Set your minds on what is above, not on what is on the earth."

Now Christianly, this is what we are to do! But humanly, selfishly, we are still on that human side saying and asking the questions: Why did this happen? Why couldn't I have five more minutes? One more Sunday service? How does someone go to looking good to you being summoned to speak at the funeral?

Then something amazing happens! You are reminded of something Ronnie mumbled to you in the hospital. Yes, Ronnie, the one you are having all this emotion and love for. And he reminds you as you are praying over him with family and singing songs of praise and worship, that he will see you again!

Now you might be thinking of the Carrie Underwood song, but the reminder is from a passage of Psalms 23 which says,

> *The LORD is my shepherd;*
> *there is nothing I lack.*
> *He lets me lie down in green pastures;*
> *He leads me beside quiet waters.*
> *He renews my life;*
> *He leads me along the right paths*
> *for His name's sake.*
> *Even when I go through the darkest valley,*

I fear no danger,

for You are with me;

Your rod and Your staff —they comfort me.

You prepare a table before me

in the presence of my enemies;

You anoint my head with oil;

my cup overflows.

Only goodness and faithful love will pursue me

all the days of my life,

and I will dwell in the house of the LORD

as long as I live.

Even though he cannot say it in words, Ronnie refers you to a scripture and number so you can try to understand this and be reminded by him but also reminded by a higher power than ourselves. Hey, listen to me, "Even when I go through the darkest valley, I fear no danger."

When we are to the point where we are about to have someone depart from us, yes, we are in that same valley of the shadow of death with them, but with them we will not fear! We will not reflect on the fact that things are going to be different now at home, work, or even church.

We will reflect on moments like on that day when the nurse asked Ronnie, "Who's the president of the United States?" and he answered, "Jimmy Carter!" The nurse said, "Wait, what? Now come on now, are you messing with me? It has a B in it." And the next answer he gave was "Donald be trump!" And you were trying to be professional, but all you could do is fall over and laugh. You hear his final answer to the question, which was "Oh, it's Joey Biden!" And you see that crooked smile on his face, you are just laughing out loud falling over, thinking to yourself we are going to be asked to leave.

We will reflect on the passage from Proverbs 3:5-6 which says,

Trust in the LORD with all your heart,

and do not rely on your own understanding;

think about Him in all your ways,

and He will guide you on the right paths.

We will acknowledge that yes, this hurts! But imagine the laughter he is having right this moment! Imagine the smile he has on now at being with Jesus, and with a bonus blessing at seeing his mother, father, wife, and many others that have called out and submitted to the one and only Jesus Christ, the Son of God!

Imagine the day you fully put your whole heart and trust in the hands of Jesus Christ and you asked Him to become your Lord and Savior. Imagine seeing the doors of Heaven opening up with Jesus running toward you saying, "Well done. good and faithful servant!"

We will also acknowledge the fact that not only ourselves but the whole congregation has now another job of making disciples. Taking Ronnie's passion, job, calling, and memory, carrying it forward and beyond. Some ways he did this that you can too:

1. Tell someone about Jesus, even speaking a different language to someone who does not speak English.
2. Ask someone at McDonald's if you can pray for them, then going back four weeks later and saying, "Oh, hey! How is that loved one we prayed about?"
3. Split half of your sandwich with the person mowing your lawn, even if it is a small meal.

Maybe you have some of that humanness going on. Maybe you have something so big that is in your heart, you are to the point where you want to scream! But deep down, you know that you have got to be better than what you want to say!

First, I am going to ask you to let God take it from you! Yes, surrender all the emotions, whether it be guilt, anger, sadness, etc.

Second, I want to encourage and remind you that maybe you never asked Jesus Christ into your heart. Or maybe you are calling yourself a Christian, but you just fully understood the whole meaning today! If so, I am going to ask that you reach out to me, because I would love to help you get started on that journey.

And finally, please play "I Will See You Again" by Carrie Underwood and imagine how it will feel to see our loved ones again and being able to see Jesus in the flesh!

Let us pray:

> *Dear Heavenly Father, Lord Jesus, we thank You for the many years, months, or even days we have had with either our father, brother, friend, mentor, or chaplain. Lord Jesus, we no longer mourn but rejoice in You that Mr. Ronnie has finally come home to You! Lord Jesus, if there is any out there today that do not know You personally or have slipped away from the Christian life, we ask that You remind them how much they are loved and cared for and how only You and You alone can fill the emptiness inside a person. We ask Lord Jesus that if there are any others in a similar situation today that You give them the strength and the peace and mercy to get through it. We ask that You watch over us and again that You will be with our hearts and minds. We also thank You for the power of prayer! Forgive us of our sins. In Jesus' name we pray. Amen!*

I love you, Ronnie! You run along. "And you go rest high on that mountain."

LIFE LESSON SERMONS

Even before I thought about writing *Cheezey* or this book, people asked about my Life Lesson Sermons being published. While I have shared funeral sermons, like the one in the last chapter for Ronnie and for Walt Knowles in my first book, I do not know when I'll get around to pulling all my Life Lesson Sermons together. But I wanted to share three here with you, once again edited for brevity.

THE HOLE

Please pause for a moment of silence to honor those who have served and who have made the ultimate sacrifice.

Let us pray:

> *Dear Heavenly Father, Lord Jesus, we thank You for this day. Lord Jesus, we also thank You for Your love, mercy, grace, healing, peace, forgiveness, patience, Word, and much more. Lord Jesus, we also thank You for allowing people to keep us safe, and we ask that You will be with them and their family and that You will also be with their hearts and minds. Lord Jesus, as we study Your Word today, please be with our hearts and minds and allow us to bring more of Your message out to the world. Forgive us of our sins. In Jesus' name we pray. Amen!*

The Bible I am reading out of is the HCSB. Our Scripture reading comes from Jonah 1:1-17, which says,

> The word of the LORD came to Jonah son of Amittai: "Get up! Go to the great city of Nineveh and preach against it, because their wickedness has confronted Me." However,

Jonah got up to flee to Tarshish from the LORD's presence. He went down to Joppa and found a ship going to Tarshish. He paid the fare and went down into it to go with them to Tarshish, from the LORD's presence.

Then the LORD hurled a violent wind on the sea, and such a violent storm arose on the sea that the ship threatened to break apart. The sailors were afraid, and each cried out to his god. They threw the ship's cargo into the sea to lighten the load. Meanwhile, Jonah had gone down to the lowest part of the vessel and had stretched out and fallen into a deep sleep.

The captain approached him and said, "What are you doing sound asleep? Get up! Call to your god. Maybe this god will consider us, and we will not perish."

"Come on!" the sailors said to each other. "Let us cast lots. Then we will know who is to blame for this trouble we are in." So, they cast lots, and the lot singled out Jonah. Then they said to him, "Tell us who is to blame for this trouble we are in. What is your business and where are you from? What is your country and what people are you from?"

He answered them, "I am a Hebrew. I worship Yahweh, the God of the heavens, who made the sea and the dry land."

Then the men were even more afraid and said to him, "What is this you've done?" The men knew he was fleeing from the LORD's presence, because he had told them. So they said to him, "What should we do to you to calm this sea that's against us?" For the sea was getting worse and worse.

He answered them, "Pick me up and throw me into the sea so it may quiet down for you, for I know that I'm to blame for this violent storm that is against you." Nevertheless, the men rowed hard to get back to dry land, but they could not because the sea was raging against them more and more.

So they called out to the LORD: "Please, Yahweh, do not let us perish because of this man's life, and do not charge us with innocent blood! For You, Yahweh, have done just as You pleased." Then they picked up Jonah and threw him into the sea, and the sea stopped its raging. The men feared the LORD even more, and they offered a sacrifice to the LORD and made vows.

Now the LORD had appointed a huge fish to swallow Jonah, and Jonah was in the fish three days and three nights.

Have any of y'all ever had a parent or grown up say, "You are digging your hole deeper and deeper!" Many times in life, we get ourselves in holes. The holes we dig or sink ourselves into can range from the tiniest problem to a full-blown hole. Here we see the prophet Jonah get himself not just into a hole but a fish! In verses 1-3, Jonah had orders from the Lord to go to this great city. While he was there, he was to preach against all their sins, in front of God's eyes. Now, instead of following orders from God, Jonah let his fear get the best of him.

As Christians, when God asks us to do something, we do it. Now, we have a choice to listen to God or ignore God. But when it comes to God giving orders, we should not pick and choose what orders we are to follow! I do not care how fast you run, how fast you drive, how good you are at hide-and-seek because we cannot outrun, out strength, out drive, or out hide God! He is always on scene with us even when we do not see Him. He is there. Can I please get an Amen?!

Verses 4-6: God had thrown a storm upon the sea, with violent winds so strong that the ship was going to break apart. The sailors were afraid and each one of them was calling out to his god. Imagine it being 2023 with these sailors on the boat. You have many people with different beliefs and different views on religion. Now each one of the sailors are asking their god to help them out, but no one is home to answer. They began unloading the cargo to make the ship's journey through this storm a little better, but even that did not help. Jonah had fallen into a deep sleep downstairs in the lowest part of the boat. It must have been pretty low for him not to hear it. The captain of the ship went down and told him to get up and call out to his God, thinking that maybe his God could help so they would not die.

Verses 7-9: The sailors seem to think there is someone to blame for this crazy storm. So they decide to cast lots to see who it is. It could mean picking the shortest straw or flipping a coin. Now, I do not know about you, but that is a strange way of doing it. What if it had gone to the captain and he was not the source? But it seems they had their lots cast out on Jonah! They start questioning him, wanting to know who is to blame, what he is doing on the ship, and where he is from. Jonah admits his wrongs and takes responsibility for his actions. He tells them that he is a Hebrew, and he worships Yahweh, meaning God.

Verses 10-13: After Jonah tells them his information, the people on the ship started getting even more scared! They started questioning him even further, finding out that he was fleeing from God's presence. They asked what they could do to make this right and save the ship and themselves. Jonah tells them to toss him overboard and it may quiet down. Jonah owned up to his mistake, saying how he knew he was to blame for this violent storm that is against them.

Imagine being there in that situation and hearing that! You are told to basically take a life so you may live and save yourself. These sailors were trying everything they could so they would not have to throw Jonah over. That moment right there is having a heart!

Verses 14-17: Seeing no other choice, they cried out to the Lord! They asked for mercy and not to be charged for getting ready to take Jonah's life to save their own. They picked Jonah up and tossed him overboard into the sea. Then everything calmed down! Then these guys seem to have a turning point in their faith. They saw God's wrath but then saw His peace! So, each man offered a sacrifice to the Lord and made vows to Him. As for Jonah, he did not die. But God did allow Jonah to be swallowed up by a fish. He remained there for three days and three nights, but alive. It was there in the belly of the fish where Jonah got right with God and prayed to Him!

In Jonah 2:1-2 it says,

> *Jonah prayed to the LORD his God from inside the fish:*
> *"I called to the LORD in my distress,*
> *and He answered me.*
> *I cried out for help in the belly of Sheol;*
> *You heard my voice."*

After getting right with God, God commanded the fish, and the fish vomited Jonah out on dry land!

What hole have you gotten yourself into? Better yet, what fish have you gotten yourself into? Maybe you have gotten angry with God and have not spoken to Him in a while. Maybe you have a broken heart from a broken relationship, and you have not fully healed from it. Maybe you have found yourself in a hole dealing with some kind of addiction. Maybe you have found yourself feeling guilty because you have not been living, acting, fighting, or even speaking like a Christian.

If we go back to the first part of this Scripture, we see,

> *The word of the LORD came to Jonah son of Amittai: "Get*
> *up! Go to the great city of Nineveh and preach against it,*
> *because their wickedness has confronted Me."*

homosexuality

When we look around the world, even here in our backyard of America, there is so much sin. When we hear, "It's okay for a man to be with a man and a woman to be with a woman," or "It's okay for a woman to become a man and a man to become a woman," people have chosen to take the easy way out and support this poisonous lie so they can avoid conflict instead of standing up for God and handling it in a godly way. Or people in the churches mislead people by telling them this poisonous lie is okay, and slap and spit on God's Word!

Same thing with abortion. God wants to give life, but people murder His creation and throw honor and God in the trash! They take away an opportunity for people that have a God-given love and gift for taking care of children but are unable to have a child. A child that could have been adopted is instead taken away from the world. Instead of calmly discussing, we fight and murder. We may not do it physically but in our minds, words, and hearts we do.

When a fallen brother or sister has fallen into a hole, instead of helping, we tend to bury them deeper. In Ecclesiastes 4:9-10 it says,

> *Two are better than one because they have a good reward*
> *for their efforts. For if either falls, his companion can lift*
> *him up; but pity the one who falls without another to lift*
> *him up.*

Whatever hole you have gotten yourself into or whatever fish you might find yourself into, I want you to know no matter what your situation is, God loves you! He loved us so much that He came down into human standards. I said it before, and I will say it again, Jesus is God in human form! He paid the price and died for all of our sins so that we could be free from our holes and chains and fish!

I cannot promise we will have bright and shiny days! I cannot promise we will be sin-free because we are sinners saved by grace! But I promise if you make Jesus Christ your Lord and Savior, Jesus will allow you to be free from being in a hell hole and heading to the streets of glory!

You may say, "Chaplain Cheese, I raised my hand when I was younger but I fully understand now what it means to be a Christian!" Or you may have grown up in a religious home but you want to go from world religion to a personal relationship with Jesus Christ! If that is you, with head bowed and eyes closed, let us pray:

> *Dear Lord Jesus, we thank You for allowing us to once again study Your Word. Lord Jesus, we rejoice in You for any decision that was made here and we ask that You will allow us to take Your message out into the world. We ask Lord Jesus that You will be with us this week and that You will be with our family and our friends! Forgive us of our sins. In Jesus' name we pray. Amen!*

I AM CHEEZEY

Let us pray:

> *Dear Lord Jesus, we thank You for this day. Lord Jesus, we ask that You will be with all of the hurt in the world right now, and Lord Jesus, we thank You for Your mercy, grace, blood, forgiveness, Word, love, wisdom, compassion, and blessings. Lord Jesus, we thank You for allowing us to be here tonight. We ask that You will be with our hearts and minds. Forgive us of our sins. In Jesus' name we pray. Amen.*

The Bible I am reading out of is the HCSB. Our Scripture reading is from John 1:40-42, which says,

> Andrew, Simon Peter's brother, was one of the two who heard John and followed Him. He first found his own

> brother Simon and told him, "We have found the Messiah!"
> (which means "Anointed One"), and he brought Simon
> to Jesus.
> When Jesus saw him, He said, "You are Simon, son of John.
> You will be called Cephas" (which means "Rock").

Verses 40-42: Andrew Simon (Peter's brother) has seen and found Jesus, who is not only the Messiah but also God in human form! Andrew brings his brother to Jesus! Before Peter, he was who? Yes, he was Simon! But Jesus sees something in him and no longer calls him Simon and instead calls him Peter.

Some might say Jesus saw a different side of Peter. Some people might say that before Simon became Peter, he was the rebel (and not the good kind either). But when Jesus came into his life after really seeing who Jesus was, he no longer saw the Rebel Simon. Instead He saw this God-fearing Peter that would grow to be one of the many great messengers of Jesus Christ! Can I please get an Amen?!

I have been asked who my favorite disciple is in the Bible. It is Peter because I am Peter. Throughout the course of Peter's journey, we see him have ups and downs. We see him have many great warrior moments! But also, we see him have small bits of human fear, like when he denied Christ three times. Some might even call the things Peter did impulsive! Now, I get called out doing that from time to time, and I do not like it, because to me, people are calling me incompetent and that is one thing I am not! I can and will admit that sometimes I do act without thinking, but I learned through moments in my own walk in the fire service and other events in my life, sometimes if you think instead of doing it, you die!

Some of you think that might be harsh, but it is the truth! Acting impulsively is what Peter was known for in the course of his life. So, you know what? Maybe Peter is autistic! Many of you might laugh at that, but I am really serious! Out of these twelve disciples, Peter is different! I know many of us have different eyes, ears, noses, we even have different views and opinions on things. But from my point of view, Peter is smart! He sees little details about Jesus other people miss.

In Matthew 16:13-20 it says,

> *When Jesus came to the region of Caesarea Philippi, He asked His disciples, "Who do people say that the Son of Man is?"*
>
> *And they said, "Some say John the Baptist; others, Elijah; still others, Jeremiah or one of the prophets."*
>
> *"But you," He asked them, "who do you say that I am?"*
>
> *Simon Peter answered, "You are the Messiah, the Son of the living God!"*
>
> *And Jesus responded, "Simon son of Jonah, you are blessed because flesh and blood did not reveal this to you, but My Father in heaven. And I also say to you that you are Peter, and on this rock, I will build My church, and the forces of Hades will not overpower it. I will give you the keys of the kingdom of heaven, and whatever you bind on earth is already bound in heaven, and whatever you loose on earth is already loosed in heaven."*
>
> *And He gave the disciples orders to tell no one that He was the Messiah.*

Verses 13-14: Jesus asks His disciples who people say He is, and these disciples tell him.

Verses 15-20: He switches the question to who they say He is. It does not say if anybody else gave an answer or how fast Peter answered. But Peter said, "You are the Messiah the Son of the Living God!" In that moment, it was not time for Jesus to die yet, so He gave orders for them not to tell.

Again y'all, Jesus is God in human form! It was not how many years you have to go to college to be ordained, it was not from the local news tip that says, "Hey y'all, this just in. God blessed Peter by giving him common sense and Heavenly knowledge to see God in human form."

What comes to mind when you think of church? The wrong answer would be a building with windows and doors. Y'all, the number one answer is *we* are the church, God's flock! Peter was one of God's churches! God's church is not made up of 4x4s and cinder block. It has been made up as a church on wheels, feet, and shoes!

Being who Jesus is and knowing what He knows probably made Peter uneasy when Jesus said, "And not even death will overcome it." Peter is this big Christian rock among the church, but one day in the final moments in his mission for Jesus Christ, Peter would die. Not just on a cross but upside down on a cross. But Jesus already had the keys of Heaven, for it was His blood, His sacrifice, and His own death on the Cross that would be poured out for every person who confessed Jesus Christ as their Lord and Savior and who asked Him to forgive them of their sins and asked Him to come into their hearts to be saved! Yall, with Jesus Christ, salvation is here! Can I please get an Amen?!

When we lose our life in whatever way it happens, which every one of us is dying right now as we speak, one day those of us who have asked Jesus Christ into our hearts we will be called home! Because whoever got Jesus will refine their life in Him even if we die! Can I get an Amen?!

I said earlier that I am Peter, but it is only in a different name and style. Growing up in Pineville, I was called Steven, just plain old Steven. If you asked my brother, mama, or any of my six or seven so-called brothers and sisters I had back then if they would trust me with a gun, or put their life in my hands and ask me to risk my life to save theirs, or give me with a truck and a four-wheeler, they would say no!

Earlier in the sermon, I said, "Some might say Jesus saw a different side of Peter. Some people might say that before Simon became Peter, he was the rebel (and not the good kind either). But when Jesus came into his life after really seeing who Jesus was, he no longer saw the Rebel Simon. Instead He saw this God-fearing Peter that would grow to be one of the many great messengers of Jesus Christ!"

I became Cheeseburger around middle school. But to me, I was still hiding under the name Rebel Steven just like Simon was Rebel Simon. I was baptized at a young age, but in 2012 I fully gave my heart to Jesus Christ. That is when I fully went from being Rebel Steven (Simon) to Cheeseburger (Peter).

Now, like Peter, I still have my own struggles and moments where I trip and fall, and I do go without thinking sometimes and end up getting somewhat burned in ways I really should not have to explain. But some of the ways I have been burned in life, I can honestly live with those scars, even as a firefighter chaplain. And please do not get me wrong, I am still a rebel at heart. I just do it with more of a different cheezey style and form!

Back when I was Rebel Steven, my youth group leader and Sunday school teacher wrote this to me: "As a guy who used to teach him in youth group in church, I can definitely say this guy has been transformed by God. Cheese, you have gone from a tornado of a kid and a thug wannabe who was trying to figure out who you are, to someone who has a ministry and a calling from God. And on top of that, a published book! I pray God keeps using you in big ways. "

Back in the day, I would not sit still! I would be bouncing off the walls until either Mama or one of her daughters would make me settle down! Oh yes, Rebel Steven (Simon) was in his own little world. But then, when God had my full attention and I fully gave Him my whole heart, I became Cheeseburger (Peter). Now many years down the road, here I am on scene as a Christian, self-employed lawn-care worker, prayer warrior, inactive ordained firefighter chaplain, lead church security guard, storm chaser/storm spotter, hunter, driver with a learner's permit, author, autistic, award winner, certified and accommodated under my rank.

I have put my life and limbs on the line to help save someone's life. People reach out to me and say, "Chaplain Cheese! Please pray for me! I need you." Some people drive around looking for me just so I can stop working in the hot sun to say a prayer for them and their family!

Back in the day, Rebel Steven used to just say, "I will pray for you." I'd let them go away, still with a broken heart, probably wondering if I'd even remember to pray later. As Cheeseburger, I learned that it is better and makes huge difference to pray for someone right there on scene.

Many people want to label me as some kind of hero, but I never wanted that title at all! Ever! I just wanted to be cheezey, the way God made me! But now I see people want to question and underestimate me and my ability to handle certain situations. Okay then, corner me, underestimate and question my ability to do my job, dishonor and disrespect my name and current rank, even dishonor my views and let others wear their views on their wrist!

You can try to lock me in a cage and try to put a brand-new style on me, but I have been cornered before, and I did not go speechless the last time, and I certainly will not go speechless this time. I will do what I always do, wear what I want to wear, lift my hands up to Heaven and bow my head and soar and burn across the sky on the wings of an eagle, who is also my Lord and Savior Jesus Christ, and remain cheezey! Because it will only make my story that much cheezier.

I can sit there and try to change people's views on me, instead I will let the Lord our God sort it out!

In 1 Timothy 4:11-16, Paul says in a letter to Timothy:

> *Command and teach these things. Let no one despise your youth; instead, you should be an example to the believers in speech, in conduct, in love, in faith, in purity. Until I come, give your attention to public reading, exhortation, and teaching.*
>
> *Do not neglect the gift that is in you; it was given to you through prophecy, with the laying on of hands by the council of elders. Practice these things; be committed to them, so that your progress may be evident to all. Pay close attention to your life and your teaching; persevere in these things, for by doing this you will save both yourself and your hearers.*

Often people want to change your style with the way you come around with the Gospel. But if you feel the style that you're being told to be is not who God wants you to be, then do not do it! Because once we start being someone we are not, not only will we hurt and let ourselves and others down, but we will also be hurting and letting God down.

Even if it stops me from getting a new rank in the future, the ranks that God has for me down the road will be cheezey, but the biggest and cheeziest rank will be waiting above in Heaven on the streets of glory!

If you have not been listening, then please listen now . . . I am cheezey today, I am cheezey tomorrow, and I am cheezey when God calls me home.

Each of us has a Peter in our own lives, who points us to verses or prayers by just being there. They do not do it by pretending to be someone they are not. They do not do it because they are being made a new rank. They do it by the style God wants them to, which is by His will!

If there is anyone interested in being a Christian or in rededicating their life to Jesus Christ, please reach out to me! I would love to pray and help y'all get started on that journey.

Let us pray:

> *Dear Lord Jesus, we thank You for this day, and we thank You for the power of prayer. Lord Jesus, here today we ask that You allow us to take Your Word as You want us to and to be. We ask that You will be with is this weekend and we also ask that You be with the brokenhearted. Forgive us of our sins. In Jesus' name we pray. Amen.*

REMEMBERING 9/11

Let us pray:

> *Dear Heavenly Father, Lord Jesus, here today we honor the lives that were lost on September 11, 2001. Lord Jesus, we ask that You will be with the minds and the hearts. Lord Jesus, we thank You for all of the blessings we have in this country. We also thank You for Your mercy, love, forgiveness, grace, blood, peace, hope, Word, power of prayer, strength, and much more! Lord Jesus, we ask that You will be with the families that have lost loved ones, whether it be through war or through the attacks that happened years ago. We ask that You forgive us of our sins. In Jesus' name we pray. Amen.*

It has been many years since the horrible day that left America shocked and hurt on September 11, 2001. Every now and then when I respond to a chaplain call or when I am ministering to a person, people ask, "Chaplain Cheese, why do so many bad things happen to so many good people?" Or "Why does God allow stuff like 9/11 to happen?"

If we look back in Genesis, you will understand. If we had perfect days—I mean perfect, like days full of rest, no war, no death, and no sin—then what was the point of God sending Jesus on scene to help save the world?

The Bible I am reading from is the HCSB. Jesus says, in John 16:33,

> *I have told you these things so that in Me you may have peace. You will have suffering in this world. Be courageous! I have conquered the world.*

Jesus reminds not only His disciples but also us, that yes, there will be suffering in this world. But our peace is found with the Conqueror, the Champion, our Lord and Savior, Jesus Christ! And the Champ says, "Be courageous! For I have conquered the world."

Yes, Jesus died on the Cross but was raised three days later! He took the punishment for our sins and took them to the grave, and after three days He returned with brighter grace, love, and mercy. Can I please get an Amen?!

Instead of turning the date into a holiday off from school, have the students write a report of what they learned from the events, then before school lets out, look at the US flag and have a moment of silence and prayer. But that is just my view. How do you plan to honor the fallen? How do you plan to honor America on this day?

Will you think of someone who fought for you? Will you think about the empty seats that are among many at Thanksgiving and Christmas? Will you think about the servicemen and women? Will you think about the heroes that fought back trying to prevent more terror from happening? And last, will you think about your own personal relationship with Jesus Christ?

We have peace and more freedom than you can imagine! But it is found in the only one true God, which is our Lord and Savior Jesus Christ.

You say you're tired of the hurt and pain, and I cannot promise you sunny days from here on out, but I promise if you ask Jesus Christ to come into your heart, you will see glory upon the streets of glory!

Y'ALL CAN'T KEEP ME DOWN

1 Samuel 16:7 says,

> But the LORD said to Samuel, "Do not look at his appearance or his stature, because I have rejected him. Man does not see what the LORD sees, for man sees what is visible, but the LORD sees the heart."

People often look at me, as an:

Autistic firefighter chaplain

Autistic self-employed lawn-care worker

Autistic church security leader guard

Autistic author

Autistic storm chaser

Autistic Christian

Autistic prayer warrior

Autistic hunter

Autistic driver

Autistic deacon

Everything they see they put the word autistic in front of it. The Autistic guy, still having awards, certifications, and accommodations under his rank.

And yes, I do joke about my autism. But other people see it as a weakness. They see themselves as big mighty warriors on the field of battle, but when I come up on scene to check on them, they look at me as a weak, little shepherd boy. Like everyone did with David.

Many people want to tell me, "Cheese that's untrue and not fair." You're right, it is not fair, but you're also wrong because it is true. Often people are a Hollywood Christian to my face. They act one way then go behind my back and doubt and insult me. When called by God to become a brand-new deacon for the church, word got back to me of what was said. In some people's defense, they were only looking after me, and that is okay, because I can handle that but still keep moving forward.

But others insulted me by saying, "Let's make him a junior deacon or a deacon in training." That right there, back in the day, I would have mishandled the situation. You would hear from me, but not in the Christian way. Like my former youth leader and Sunday school teacher Josh Walker said, I was a tornado of a kid! I have grown so much.

So, instead of the old Steven Simon. You will get to see Cheeseburger Peter as well as David, speaking here to that Goliath: Junior deacon, huh? Calling me a junior deacon is basically calling me a junior firefighter. I assure you, I am not a child and I am not a junior. You think you know me? My name is Firefighter Chaplain 79 Steven J. "Cheeseburger" Struble. I am thirty-two years old. Before I was a firefighter chaplain, even before I became a deacon, I was already acting as one. I would check in with people. If someone needed prayer, I would pray for them. If someone needed advice on how to handle a situation, I would give them God's Word and my two cents. Even before I was standing behind a pulpit or standing among a prayer group, God was having me write sermons.

The good Lord knows I am not perfect. I know who I am. I know what I am. I am what you are. I am what the world is. Which is sinners saved by the grace of God. In Romans 3:23-24, Paul says,

> *For all have sinned and fall short of the glory of God. They are justified freely by His grace through the redemption that is in Christ Jesus.*

In Romans 5:8, Paul also says,

> *But God proves His own love for us in that while we were*
> *still sinners, Christ died for us!*

There are many other passages and verses in the Bible that I could bring up, but I think you can see the message, at least I pray you do. I, along with everyone else, have issues with sin. We even sin every day. Sometimes we do not even know we are sinning. Lord knows what all I have been through. I might even be the disciple Peter's twin. We are all sinners saved by the grace of God. Can I please get an Amen?!

But you see, that is the beauty of it all, isn't it? Have you ever spilled or made a stain on something? God is the ultimate 409, Dawn, Bleach, Goo Gone, Downy Rinse and Refresh—and all of that has one name that is known to the world! Our Lord and Savior Jesus Christ! Even when we fall and trip, He cleans us off and sends us on our way.

Even as Christians we tend to be Hollywood Christians. We do not mean to, but we do. It is a funny thing about actors, because I have been dealing with actors my whole life. They may have rejected me and disowned me, laughed in my face, made fun of me, gone out with me just to use me to get to someone else, questioned me and what I can and cannot do, doubted my roles, looked at me as just some glorified mascot, thought they were better than me just because they had a driver's license, etc.

In God's Word, it says in Jeremiah 5:21,

> *Hear this,*
> *you foolish and senseless people.*
> *They have eyes, but they do not see.*
> *They have ears, but they do not hear.*

If you cannot understand it, I can make it clear for you by just saying this: You cannot keep me down! The comments, the worldly act, may hurt me. I know who I truly am. I am a child of God who is like Peter!

When it was brought to my attention what was said about me, I was upset and hurt, I am not going to lie about it. But like everything else, I do what I need to do, and I keep moving forward.

By the way, thanks for making my story even cheezier. On Sunday, August 27, 2023, I was ordained as a deacon.

AUTISM

I have many titles. In addition, I have a blessing by God of autism. You see, my mama was a single parent for a long time, raising my brother and myself. She had help from God and family and friends. I learned a lot over the years, and one is that there are two ways to look at autism.

You can let it beat you, let it make you a prisoner. You can force yourself to pretend you do not have it, thinking you're better than everyone else, and when help comes around, refuse it. This only gets you halfway in life.

Or you can "beat" autism by embracing it. You can break free from those chains and embrace it as a gift from God. You might have to wait many years to do certain things or work harder than others may have to, but it will happen.

I wanted to be a storm chaser, so I searched the web and made calls and got certified by the grace of God. I always wanted to join the military, and that door was shut only to be opened back up, not as a Marine sniper or K9 handler, but as a volunteer firefighter. Even when I wasn't looking for it, God opened the door Himself. I had always wanted to drive but thought it would never happen until, after years with health battles, God presented me with the opportunity. I may have roadblocks here and there, but if I did not have roadblocks, my life would be easy. Where is the fun in that? And beyond all that, God blessed me and called me as a firefighter chaplain. I recently applied with the CMPD (Charlotte Mecklenburg Police Department) as a police chaplain. I'm still in the application process but hopefully will hear something soon.

I like the hard life because it gives me a chance to depend on God more than myself. And I have found God! I cannot really say that if my life was easy, I would be where I am now. Probably not. The way I look at it, God made it possible. In reality, the only being that can shut the door fully is the Lord our God.

People look at me as a mascot for autism, and that is not what I am or who I was. Autism is different for everyone who has it.

When people look at me, they have these smirky looks and cocky laughs. But then they hear about me risking my life to save another, whether it's facing off with someone who is suicidal or diving headfirst through a door of a moving car or assisting on a call until EMS arrives on scene. They are shocked. They say, "What are you talking about? This is Cheese we are talking about here. Cheese does not do this or cannot even do this kind of stuff."

I am not here to prove a point. I do not believe in luck. I have faced a lot of ups and downs. It is by faith, love, redemption, and the grace of God I am here and have done what I have done. Just like David, it was through God and faith that he was able to defeat the mighty Goliath. It was by faith in God and His forgiveness that David was able to find redemption for his falls.

MY IDENTITY

I could write one thousand books to try to get people to see who I am, but people are going to see me how they want to see me, and I am not going to be able to change that, no matter what I want them to see. Only God can open people's eyes and drop people's jaws to allow them to see what it is truly in front of them. I am not a hero, because I am just like everyone else God calls. Follower of Jesus Christ and child of God. I am just an instrument (I would be a drum because I am loud, proud, and southern, by the grace of God).

People often want us to be like the world, but we cannot. In my journey as a firefighter chaplain, I have lost friendships because I would not partake in a wedding ceremony, or I would not support people in a worldly false relationship. 1 John 2:15-17 says,

> *Do not love the world or the things that belong to the world.*
> *If anyone loves the world, love for the Father is not in him.*
> *For everything that belongs to the world—the lust of the*
> *flesh, the lust of the eyes, and the pride in one's lifestyle—is*
> *not from the Father, but is from the world. And the world*
> *with its lust is passing away, but the one who does God's*
> *will remains forever.*

I am not an on-the-fence chaplain, nor am I an on-the-fence Christian. There are many chaplains, pastors, and Christians that try to mean well but they take the easy way out. God never said this would be an easy life, but He always said how He would be with us to the very end of the age. I choose to walk fully with Christ.

I may have slips and falls, but my identity will always be the same: Christian Firefighter Chaplain 79 Steven James "Cheeseburger" Struble, child of God.

People want to talk about how being brave is easy. No, being scared is easy. But being brave is the hardest. But here is the beauty of it all: Being scared allows us to find a tighter grip on faith, hope, love, mercy, peace, and much more through our Lord and Savior Jesus Christ. Being brave allows us to trust God even more! But the bonus of that is we are able to show others what God can and will do if we only trust and surrender our lives to Him.

It will not always be easy, but once you start being brave, you will be able to balance life a little better, because you will know how to trust and depend on God, no matter what the call or situation is. Can I please get an Amen?!

CLEARING THIS CALL

Since *Cheezey*, my life has been cheezier. I have learned the hard way the effects and dangers of suicide and PTSD. The message I am trying to get across in this book is that each of us really and truly has a story! And you may or may not believe it, but God is in the story whether or not you have a personal relationship with Him through Jesus Christ. Whatever you have seen, been through, heard, or done, Jesus Christ wants you to use it to bring others to Him.

Life has been tough for a lot of us, and I am not just speaking to Americans, I am speaking to everyone. You might be a first responder or someone in the military. Maybe you are a dispatcher, firefighter, police officer, chaplain, Marine, medic, nurse, etc. Maybe you have been struggling with stuff so deep inside that you have forgotten why you chose this profession. Or maybe you have gotten so heartbroken from the ungratefulness of other people.

But I do have hope for you. God is always near, even to the brokenhearted. Yes, stuff goes down on calls that civilians can only imagine. I know many people say we have to be strong and keep it all in until after the call. But then another call comes in, then another, then another, and soon we find all the emotion has built up.

I think one of the things that really messes us up with any call of service we assist on is the emotions we keep in. You still have this weight of burdens inside you. Where is the winding down process? Maybe you have issues at home, trying to take care of personal issues, trying to push them out of your head so you can help someone else with theirs.

We need to find time to find for rest and relaxation, and this goes not just for those on the call of duty, but everyone. How we do that is in Jesus Christ! Jesus says, in Matthew 11:28-30,

> *Come to Me, all of you who are weary and burdened, and I will give you rest. All of you, take up My yoke and learn from Me, because I am gentle and humble in heart, and you will find rest for yourselves. For My yoke is easy and My burden is light.*

When you feel like life on the job has you bound by guilt and shame, I am here to tell you to approach the Word of God and rest your mind and your heart upon His Words and He will give you the rest!

Jesus also says, In Matthew 5:13-16,

> *You are the salt of the earth. But if the salt should lose its taste, how can it be made salty? It is no longer good for anything but to be thrown out and trampled on by men.*
> *You are the light of the world. A city situated on a hill cannot be hidden. No one lights a lamp and puts it under a basket, but rather on a lampstand, and it gives light for all who are in the house. In the same way, let your light shine before men, so that they may see your good works and give glory to your Father in heaven.*

My fellow brothers and sisters, here today, I ask each of us to get up, because the Devil wants us all to sit on our tails and hide the light. But what God wants us to do is to let our light shine before men.

He wants us to go to the Gentle Giant who is hurting and remind him of the redemption, mercy, and forgiveness he has in Jesus Christ. Even if that means staying with him, risking your own safety and life when he is on edge.

He wants us to run to the elderly who has fallen to remind her no matter what age she is, she still has the freedom and the purpose to go around and live her life without the fear of falling and to remind others of God's love!

He wants us to help the gentlemen who is having issues behind the wheel, even if it means having to run full speed in cowboy boots, risking our life diving in the car to save his.

At the end of *Cheezey*, I asked, "What is your story?" But today, I ask y'all, "When will you tell your story? How will you tell your story?" It may be through a song or a book. Or it might be just through your own personal testimony of telling someone about Jesus.

Now, you may say, "Chaplain Cheese, do you know how long it will take to tell my story?" Start by telling how you came to know Jesus Christ as your own personal Savior. Let God take it from there! Whatever cracks or sadness you have, it can all be repaired by Jesus Christ!

Whether you have autism, PTSD, Down syndrome, one leg, or something else, God can and will use you! When He does, He will be using you while heads are turning and jaws are dropping wide open!

BROTHER

Before I clear this call, I wanted to speak to my step brother-in-law.

Brother, I wanted to say thank you for everything you do, not only for me but for everyone. I know many times you deal with stressful situations. But in those stressful times, you may not know it, but you somehow try to make someone better than they are and in your own way help them find Jesus Christ.

Years ago, you came into my life to become not just brothers but also best friends. You never had to do anything for me or be my friend or brother, but you took the time to get to know me, and you took the time to listen to me and give me advice. You took the time to teach me things, like how to perform submission moves and mixed martial arts. You even taught me how to shoot my first gun and took me under your wing to show me how to safely honor and respect it. When my prayer was granted and answered by God, you taught me the fundamentals of truck driving and helped prepare me for my test.

Whenever we both have stress on our jobs, we can talk to each other about it. Whenever we have those funny moments, we make the other laugh. You give me advice and you also allow me to give you advice on things. I know when I have questions about how to handle a call or how to handle a situation better, you always seem to find the right solution.

And one day I do look forward to moving out into the country up there and working full time with you and finding our own adventures or troubles. You have gone way above and beyond, but I thank you. Though we are not fully blood related as brothers, know that you will always be my brother. I thank you for all that you do in my life.

FINAL PRAYER

Let us pray:

Dear Heavenly Father, Lord Jesus, I thank you once again for allowing me to spread Your Word through another book. Lord Jesus, I pray for all of the readers that are reading this right now, I pray that You will remove any stress or pain that they might be having right now. Lord Jesus, instead of someone taking their story away, allow them to be able to soar on Your peace, love, mercy, grace, blood, forgiveness, mercy, and more so they may be able to give their story to others and even help someone else find You in it. We ask that You will be with all of my fellow first responders, whether it be dispatch, fire, medic, police, military, nurse, security, and more. We also ask that You will be with all of the rest of Your children of this world.
We thank You for the power of prayer and we ask that You forgive us of our sins. In Jesus' name we pray. Amen!

Firefighter Chaplain 79 to Central, Firefighter Chaplain 79 is clear and available.

ACKNOWLEDGMENTS

I want to thank my Lord and Savior Jesus Christ for making me cheezier and for all of the many blessings I have been given. I would also like to thank my mama and all of the rest of my family and friends.

Special thanks once again to my editor, Mrs. Kyle Marie McMahon, for helping me with yet another book. Also to Jason Huey for encouraging me to write again. Lieutenant Firefighter Chaplain Tommy Nieman for always training me and teaching me to be a humble firefighter chaplain, not only down here on earth but for also the kingdom of Heaven. Anyone reading this book should check out his books, *Sirens for the Cross* and *Rookie Rescuer*, and visit his website www.RookieRescuer.com.

I would like to thank the CMPD, fellow first responders Johnny Hill, Greg Clark, Scott Hermans, David Green, Bob Foster, Guerry Scott, Jon Clary, Kyle Haldeman and family, Officer Harb, Officer Randy, Officer Heather Kimal, public safety dispatcher Chris Enyart, former US Marine Chris McConnell, Chief Hudgens, TJ Whitley, Jonathan Willams, Keith Helms, Amanda Makenzie, Katie Williams, Patsy Davis, Chaplain Honaker, and Chief Trexler. To others that were missed, sorry, but thank y'all for all your love and support.

Britney Morris, my friend, I am so happy God allowed us to come back and also be part of each other's lives. I am so proud of the family God has allowed you to make. I pray that you continue to seek His Word and Will. And I look forward to seeing where God leads y'all next. I will keep on doing prayer check-ins with y'all and will continue to always be a good friend to you and your family. Keep having that smile, and always keep holding God's light and Word close to your heart. And always, keep moving forward no matter what.

Jasmine Lee, you are God sent! Keep on being you and do not ever change the way you are unless God wants you to. Keep that smile and keep on moving forward and sharing God's love and message. Congrats on your accomplishments so far, and I look forward to seeing where God leads you further.

Thanks also to Katherine Hornsby, Jimmy Beasley and family, Gentle Giant and family, Joey Wheeler, Marcus Ashworth, Shea Gladden and family, Josh Walker, the Carter Family, the Heefner family, Van Phillps, Mr. Junior and Mrs. Donna Helms, the Lamb family, the Shackleford family, the Culp family, the Gilbert family, the Rummage family, the Hopkins family, and the Davis family.

I would like to thank Mr. Alan Conklin of WBTV. Thanks for helping make me a better storm chaser and spotter, sir.

Thank you to my cousin Jennifer who made the custom t-shirts for my first book release event. If you are looking for a custom-made t-shirt, choose her!

All of my friends and others that were missed, sorry, and thank y'all though. And thanks to the many who have helped me with this book. I had many other blessings by God through the people that He brought into my life. If I keep going on with this, this list will never end, so just this last one . . . Shea, I love you sis, and I am so very proud of you!